The Candy Maker's Guide A Collection of Choice Recipes for Sugar Boiling • Fletcher Manufacturing Company

Publisher's Note

Purchase of this book entitles you to a free trial membership in the publisher's book club at www.rarebooksclub.com. (Time limited offer.) Simply enter the barcode number from the back cover onto the membership form on our home page. The book club entitles you to select from millions of books at no additional charge. You can also download a digital copy of this and related books to read on the go. Simply enter the title or subject onto the search form to find them.

Note: This is an historic book. Pages numbers, where present in the text, refer to the first edition of the book. The table of contents or index may also refer to them.

If you have any questions, could you please be so kind as to consult our Frequently Asked Questions page at www.rarebooksclub.com/faqs.cfm? You are also welcome to contact us there.

Publisher: General Books LLC™, Memphis, TN, USA, 2012. ISBN: 9781153825368.

Credits: Distributed Proofreaders.

THE CANDY MAKER'S GUIDE

A COLLECTION OF

CHOICE RECIPES FOR SUGAR BOILING

COMPILED AND PUBLISHED BY

THE FLETCHER MNF'G. CO.

MANUFACTURERS OF

Confectioners' and Candy Makers' Tools and Machines

TEA AND COFFEE URNS

BAKERS' CONFECTIONERS AND HOTEL SUPPLIES

IMPORTERS AND DEALERS IN

PURE FRUIT JUICES, FLAVORING EXTRACTS, FRUIT OILS, ESSENTIAL OILS, MALT EXTRACT, XXXX GLUCOSE, Etc.

Prize Medal and Diploma awarded at Toronto Industrial Exhibition 1894, for General Excellence in Style and Finish of our goods.

440-442 YONGE ST.,—TORONTO, CAN.

TORONTO
J JOHNSTON PRINTER & STATIONER 105 CHURCH ST
1896

FLETCHER MNF'G. CO.

TORONTO.

Manufacturers and dealers in Generators, Steel and Copper Soda Water Cylinders, Soda Founts, Tumbler Washers, Freezers, Ice Breaking Machines, Ice Cream Refrigerators, Milk Shakers, Ice Shaves, Lemon Squeezers, Ice Cream Cans, Packing Tubs, Flavoring Extracts, Golden and Crystal Flake for making Ice Cream, Ice Cream Bricks and Forms, and every article necessary for Soda Water and Ice Cream business.

INTRODUCTION.

In presenting this selection of choice recipes for Candy Makers we have endeavored to avoid everything that is not practical and easy to understand. The recipes given are from the most experienced and notable candy makers of America and Europe, and are such, that, if followed out with care and attention will be sure to lead to success. Practice is only to be had by experiment, and little failures are overcome by constant perseverance.

After the rudiments have been thoroughly mastered, the reader has ample scope to distinguish himself in the Candy world, and will do so with patience and perseverance. We trust our patrons will look upon this work, not as a literary effort, but as instruction from a practical workman to a would-be workman.

FLETCHER MNF'G. Co.,
440 & 442 Yonge St., Toronto,
Publishers.

Manufacturers of Candy Makers Tools and Machines, and every article required in Confectionery and Candy Making.

ASK FOR OUR CATALOGUE.
[Pg 4]

SUGAR BOILING.

This branch of the trade or business of a confectioner is perhaps the most important. All manufacturers are more or less interested in it, and certainly no retail shop could be considered orthodox which did not display a tempting variety of this class. So inclusive is the term "boiled goods" that it embraces drops, rocks, candies, taffies, creams, caramels, and a number of different sorts of hand-made, machine-made, and moulded goods. It is the most ancient method of which we have any knowledge, and perhaps the most popular process of modern times; the evidence of our everyday experience convinces us that (notwithstanding the boom which heralds from time to time a new sweet, cooked in a different manner, composed of ingredients hitherto unused in business), it is the exception when such goods hold the front rank for more than a few months, however pretty, tasty, or tempting they may be, the public palate seems to fall back on those made in the old lines which, though capable of improvement, seem not to be superceded. Of the entire make of confectionery in Canada, at least two-thirds of it may be written down under the name of boiled sugar. They are undoubtedly the chief features with both manufacturers and retailers, embracing, as they do, endless [Pg 5] facilities for fertile brains and deft fingers for inventing novelties in design, manipulation, combination, and finish. Notwithstanding the already great variety, there is always daily something new in this department brought into market. Many of the most successful houses owe their popularity more to their heads than their hands, hence the importance of studying this branch in all its ramifications. The endless assortment requiring different methods for preparing and manipulating make it necessary to sub-divide this branch into sections, order and arrangement being so necessary to be thoroughly understood. *When we consider the few inexpensive tools required to make so many kinds of saleable goods, it is not to be wondered at so many retailers have a fancy to make their own toffees and such like, there is no reason why a man or woman, with ordinary patience, a willing and energetic disposition, favored with a fair amount of intelligence, should not be able to become with the aid of THIS BOOK and a few dollars for tools, fairly good sugar boilers, with a few months practice.*

There are reasons why a retail confectioner should study sugar boiling. It gives character to the business, a fascinating odour to the premises, and a general at-homeness to the surroundings. No goods look more attractive and tempting to the sweet eating public than fresh made goods of this kind. A bright window can be only so kept by makers. Grainy or sticky drops may be reboiled; scraps and what would otherwise be almost waste (at least unsightly) may be redressed in [Pg 6] another shape, and become, not only saleable, but profitable. *There are many advantages which a maker possesses over one who buys all.* For instance, clear boiled goods should be kept air tight, and are therefore delivered to the retailers in bottles, jars, or tins, on which charge is made, these have to be repacked and returned. Breakages are an important item, so is freight—the cost of the latter is saved and the former reduced to a minimum.

Whatever means are adopted to benefit the retailer and advertise the business by brighter windows, cleaner shops, less faded goods, and healthier financial conditions must contribute to the general prosperity of the trade, from the bottom step to the top rung of the ladder.

It should be the aim of all amateurs to study quality rather than price. Goods well made, carefully flavored, and nicely displayed will always command a ready sale at a fair price, giving satisfaction to the consumer and credit to the maker. Give your customers something to please the eye as well as the palate, so that every sale may be looked upon as an advertisement. Cheap, bulky, insipid stuff is unprofitable and damaging to the trade as well as to the seller. I venture to assert that more would-be makers have come to grief trying to cut each other in price for rubbishy candies than through any other cause. Look at the number of firms who have a reputation, whose very [Pg 8] [Pg 7] name command trade at good prices, year after year add to the turnover. What is the talisman? Look at their goods. There is perhaps nothing very striking in them, but they are *invariably good*, busy or slack they are made with care, packed with taste, and delivered neatly in a business-like fashion. Compare this to our makers of cheap stuff; to obtain orders they sell at unprofitable prices, often at a loss, and try to make up the difference by resorting to various methods of increasing the bulk, the result is ultimate ruin to themselves, loss to their creditors, and injury to every one concerned. Few who read these lines will not be able to verify all that is stated. The writer's advice has always been to keep up a *high degree of excellence, try to improve in every direction, and success is only a matter of patience, energy and civility.*

It is not intended to give a complete list of all kinds of candy known in the trade, that would be absurd and impossible. To be able to make any particular kind will require knowledge only to be gained by experience, so that much depends on the thoughtful endeavor of the beginner.

THE WORKSHOP.

Sugar boiling, like every other craft, requires a place to do it, fitted with tools and appliances. The requisites and requirements can be easily suited to the purse of the would-be confectioner. A work to be useful to all must cater for all, and include information which will be useful to the smaller storekeeper as well as the larger maker. To begin at the bottom, one can easily imagine a person whose only ambition is to make a little candy for the window fit for children. This could be done with a very small outlay for utensils. The next move is the purchase of a sugar boiler's furnace not very costly and certainly indispensable where quality and variety are required, it will be a great saving of time as well as money, the sugar will boil a much better color, so that cheaper sugar may be used for brown or yellow goods, while one can make acid drops and other white goods from granulated. Dutch crush, or loaf sugar, which would be impossible to make on a kitchen stove from any sort of sugar.

Fig. 2.
Steel Candy Furnace.

Fig. 206 a.
Excelsior Furnace.

No. 1—24 in. high, 19 in. diameter. Price, $7.50.
No. 2—30 in. high, 23 in. diameter. Price, $12.00.

Height 26 in., 4 holes, from 9 to 18 in. diameter. Made entirely of cast iron. Price, $16. Weight 225 lbs.

[Pg 9]

Fig. 12.
CARAMEL CUTTERS—2 Styles.
Each with Steel Shaft and Screw Handle
  No. 2—with 13 Steel Cutters, price $(
  We make this Cutter with longer rod ;
  No. 1—with 13 Tinned Cutters, price

With longer rods and any number of (

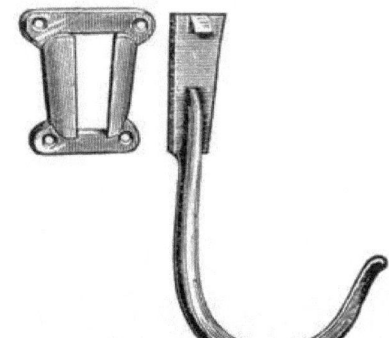

Fig. 16. Price 76c.
Improved Slide Candy Hook.

[Pg 10]

Fig. 6.
STEAM JACKET—MADE TO ORDE]

LIST OF SUGAR BOILING TOOLS REQUIRED FOR A START.

1	Candy Furnace	Price, $7 50
1	Copper Boiling pan 15×6	"	4 50
1	Candy Thermometer	"	1 75
1	Marble Slab 48×24×2	"	8 00
1	Caramel Cutter	"	6 50
1	Candy Hook	"	75
1	Pallette Knife	"	50
1	Doz. Taffy Pans	"	2 00
1	Pair English Candy	"	1 50
	Shears		
	Total		$33 00

More slab room will be required as trade increases.

We cannot go any further into the mysteries of this art successfully unless we provide ourselves with a [Pg 11] candy machine and rolls to enable us to make drops. *They are indispensable*, and if we are to go on, we must have them to enable us to make drops, and every confectioner sells drops. These machines are made to suit all classes of trade, big and little. The small ones make just as nice drops as the large ones, and will turn out in the course of a day 2 or 3 cwt., by constant use, so that for retail purposes this quantity would generally be sufficient.

Fig. 12½.
Candy Machine and Rollers for Boiled {
For Fruit Drops, Acid or Cough Drops I

These Machines are made to fit a Star of Rollers being fitted to one frame. Thu order additional rollers which will work

The Rollers are 2 in. diameter, 3⅝ in. be cut on them.

  CANDY ROLL FRAMES,
  PLAIN DROP ROLLS,
  FANCY DROP ROLLS,
[Pg 12]

Having so far got our workshop arranged the next thing is to keep it in order. Sugar boiling is dirty sticky business, especially on wet days, unless every part is kept scrupulously clean and dry, slabs and tables should be washed, no trace of sifting, scraps, or boiled goods, should be left exposed to the atmosphere during the night, the floor well swept, and a little clean sawdust put down every night.

The comfort and ease in working in a clean place far more than offsets the trouble and time it takes to put it in order, besides the goods are much drier, brighter and easier to bottle or pack. Nothing is more unpleasant than to work with sticky slabs, slimy machines or dirty scales. The boil adheres to the slabs, sticks to the rollers, spoiling the shapes, and become cloudy and spotty in weighing. We are not writing without knowledge. Any one who has worked or visited small workshops can endorse the value of these remarks, and call to mind this imaginary picture. However, there are exceptions, still the hint will be useful in a good many cases.

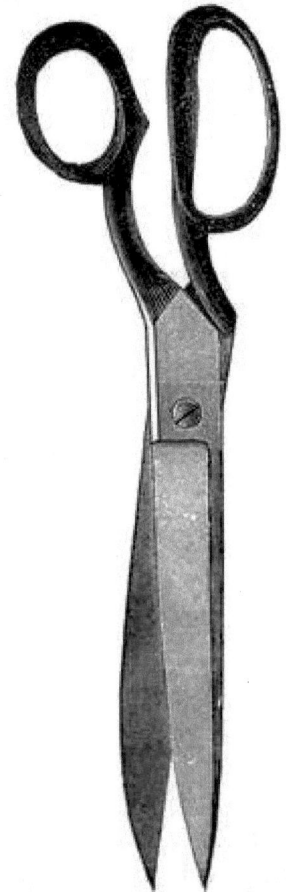

Fig. 5.
Steel Candy Shears.
English Candy Shears, $1.50.

METHOD OF SUGAR BOILING.

If the learner will study the following instructions, the author guarantees to place him in a position to boil sugar as correctly as the most experienced workman. To accomplish this, the reader should provide himself with the sugar boiler's tools named on the preceding [Pg 13] page. While the sugar is undergoing the process of boiling, it is almost impossible for a learner to determine the exact degree which the sugar has attained without a thermometer, and even the journeyman finds it so useful that you will find very few indeed who boil [Pg 14] sugar without it; in fact many of the larger shops will not allow a sugar boiler to work without one. For almost any purpose the following degrees will be found all that is necessary. For instance put into the pan in which you intend to boil, 7 lbs. granulated sugar together with one quart of water, placing it on the fire and allow it to boil. Put a cover over the pan and allow it to boil for ten minutes; then take off the cover and put the thermometer in the pan, immersing the bottom part of it in the boiling sugar, and let it remain there until the sugar is boiled to the degree you require. The following five degrees are those used by confectioners for different purposes:

Fig. 87.

1st. The smooth, viz.,—215 to 220 by the thermometer. When the mercury registers these figures the sugars may then be used for crystalizing creams, gum goods and liqueurs.

[Pg 15]

2nd. The Thread, viz., 230 and 235 is the degree which is used for making liqueurs.

3rd. The Feather, viz., 240 to 245. Only a few minutes elapse between these degrees, and the sugar must be watched closely during the boiling at this point. This degree may be used for making fondants, rich creams, cream for chocolates and fruit candying.

4th. The Ball, viz., 250 to 255. The sugar at this point is used for making cocoanut and other candies, cocoanut ice, and almost every description of grain sugar generally.

5th. The Crack, viz., 310 to 315. This is the degree which is used, with little variation, for all kinds of drops, taffies, and all clear goods, whether for the purpose of passing through machines or manipulating with the hands.

These degrees can be tested by an experienced hand without the aid of the thermometer, and the learner may accustom himself by trying them in the following manner: Take the stem of a clay pipe and dip it into the sugar as it boils, draw it out again and pass it through the forefinger and thumb; when it feels oily you will find by looking at your thermometer that it has reached the degree of smooth, 215 to 220 by the glass.

The next degree or thread, may be tried by your taking a little of the sugar off the pipe between your finger and thumb and part them gently; if you see small [Pg 16] threads hang between your finger and thumb that degree has arrived.

For the degree of Ball, 250 to 255, you must have by your hand a small jug of cold water; when you draw the pipe out of the sugar dip it in the water, and when taken out of the water, if you can work it like a piece of putty, you have got the degree of ball.

The degree of Crack must be tested the same way, and the sugar must leave the pipe clean; dip it again into cold water; when off the pipe break off a piece with your teeth; if it snaps clean in your teeth, pour your sugar on the slab at once.

NOTE.—This last degree must be tried sharply, in giving the process for trying it without the thermometer. We caution all beginners to get a thermometer, as practice alone can instruct you without. It is also necessary to state that thermometers differ a little, and should be tested.

During hot weather, it is necessary to bring the sugars up to the full degree; during winter months, the lower degrees marked will answer the purpose.

CUTTING THE GRAIN, LOWERING OR GREASING.

Almost all sugar, especially refined, whether loaf, crystalized or granulated, and most sugars known to the trade as pieces will, if boiled beyond the degree of ball, or 250 by the thermometer, when turned out of the pan becomes cloudy, then grainy, and ultimately [Pg 17] a solid lump of hard opaque sugar. To prevent this candying, as it is called several agents are used, such as glucose, cream of tartar pyroligneous acid, vinegar &c., the action of which will cause the sugar to boil clear, be pliable while hot and transparent when cold. It is therefore necessary to use some lowering agent for all boilings intended for clear goods, such as drops, taffies, rocks. &c.

Fig. 29.
Pyramid Forms.
No. 1, 22½ inch, 2 rings
Price, 90c.
No. 2, 32 inch, 3 rings
Price, $1 10.

Experience has taught most of the old hands that two of these agents possess all the merits necessary for the purpose, and are to be preferred to others for reasons it is unnecessary to state—they are cream of tartar and glucose. A great deal could be said in favor of either or both; cream of tartar is handier and cleaner to use as well as more exact in its action; goods boiled with it [Pg 18] will be a better color and, some assert, more crisp; for acids and all best and export goods it is to be recommended—use a proportion of half an ounce to every 14 lbs. of sugar—we say about, as some strong sugars require a little more, this is generally measured in a teaspoon, two spoonfuls to every 14 lbs. of sugar.

Glucose, being cheaper than sugar, is valuable to the confectioner, not only for its lowering qualities, but also as a bulk producer, *reducing the cost of the product*. On this account there is a tendency to overdo it by using too much, the result causing goods to become sticky and turn soft immediately they are exposed to the atmosphere, not only so, but we have seen drops running to a solid lump in bottles through being overdosed. If glucose is used in proper proportions, it makes an excellent lowering agent, and will answer the purpose first rate for ordinary drops and the like. Use three lbs. of glucose to every 14 lbs. of sugar; keep a panful on the furnace top, so that it will always be hot and may be easily measured by means of a saucepan or ladle holding the exact quantity; add the glucose when sugar begins to boil.

FLAVORS AND COLORS.

These form almost as important a part of the trade as the sugar itself, and it should be the chief object of every workman to try and excel in these two important features; if you do not use *good flavors*, it is a moral certainty you cannot produce *good candies*. Flavors for boiled sugars should be specially prepared, those bought at an ordinary *chemist shop may do very well for flavoring* [Pg 19] *custards and pastry, but are of no use for boiled sugars, in fact better use no essence at all, as they* are so weak that, to give the drops &c., even a slight taste the quantity required reduces the degree to which the sugar has been boiled so much that it works like putty, and sticks to the machine while being pressed through; the drops when finished look dull, dragged and stick together when bottled; tons of drops are weekly spoiled by small makers using such flavors, while a little trouble and less expense would put them out of their misery, besides giving to the goods that clear bright dry appearance to be found in the drops of a respectable house.

It must be remembered that the flavor is the very life of the candy. Color may please the eye, but excellence in that alone is not all that is required. A buyer may be attracted by the eye, but he does not eat with it. Neither old or young would knowingly eat only colored sugar. A sweet taste may be satisfied with sugar alone.

It is the variety of pleasant flavors that is desired and it is the business of the confectioner to supply it. Flavors for sugar boiling should be as concentrated as it is possible for it to be. Several large houses who have confined their attention to the wants and requirements of the confectionery and mineral water trades have succeeded in producing fruit essences of quality, which is a pleasure to work with. Being very powerful, little is required to give the boil rich flavor, consequently it passes through the machine easily, forming a perfect drop on [Pg 20] which the clear imprint of the engraving characteristic of the machine used. Essential oils used by confectioners are those having an agreeable aromatic flavor, and should be used in their original strength, without being adulterated or reduced. It is absolutely necessary that they should be pure and fresh, more particularly the oils of lemon and orange, as when not fresh and pure they partake of the flavor of turpentine, and are particularly unpleasant to the taste.

Small makers would do well to buy carefully from a good house not more than would be used up in two or three months, especially the two before mentioned. Some oils on the contrary, improve by keeping such as peppermint and lavender. All essences and oils are best kept well corked in a cool dark place.

These oils being powerful, popular and expensive, they are frequently adulterated. Cream of tartar and tartaric acid on account of the price is often increased, the former with different cheap powders, the latter usually with alum. Many people fail in the process through no fault of their own, but simply through their being supplied with inferior ingredients, it is therefore of importance, that colors and flavors should be purchased at some respectable house; get list of oils' extracts and essences from Fletcher Mnf'g. Co. who are large dealers in these goods.

The colors prepared, consisting of several very nice shades of yellow and red, also coffee brown, jetoline [Pg 21] black, damson blue, and apple green; they are in paste, ready for use, being vegetable, they are guaranteed strictly wholesome, and may be used with confidence.

WRINKLES WORTH READING ON SUGAR BOILING.

To make an acid drop to perfection, the pan must not only be clean but bright; use best white sugar, and just enough water to melt it, with a little extra cream of tartar (no glucose); boil on a sharp fire to 305; after passing through machine, well dust with icing sugar and bottle. Beginners should not try to work with less water, as the boil is more liable to grain, which can be seen by an expert and avoided. Before putting on the boil see that there is sufficient fuel on the furnace to carry through the operation. To make up a fire during the process spoils the color and quality. The sharper the sugar is boiled the better the appearance and durability.

When boiling common sugars have the pan large enough,—some throw up a good deal of foam when they reach the boiling point and are liable to flow over—watch closely, and if unable to beat the foam down, lift the pan on the side of the fire a few minutes until boiled through.

Many weak sugars burn on a clear fire before they come to a degree of crack. In this case sprinkle a little fresh fuel or ashes over the fire and replace the pan again. Should it again catch, repeat the operation nursing it up to the desired degree. Bad boiling sugar is very troublesome. A good plan is to make a rule of straining [Pg 22] the batch just after it boils, through a very fine copper wire or hair sieve, this prevents foreign matter such as grit, saw dust or even nails, which is often mixed with the sugar getting into the goods. Keep thermometer when not in use in jar of water standing on the furnace plate by the side of the pan, wash out the jar and fill with cold water every morning; keep the thermometer clean, especially the top part, as the sugar which adheres to it becomes grainy, and might spoil a whole boil. After making many dark candies thoroughly wash the thermometer before putting into a light boil.

In using colors for drops and clear goods, use them in the form of a paste where practicable, then you can mix them in when the boil is on the slab, thus saving your pan; keep the colors damp in jars, look over them every night, and, where necessary, add a little cold water to keep them moist, or the top may get dry and hard, which would make the goods specky. Use a separate piece of stick for each color to rub in with, and be careful not to use too much color; a very little goes a long way with clear boiled goods. Goods are more often spoiled by using too much than too little; more can always be added if the shades are too light, but there is no remedy if you have added too much. When coloring taffies, this must be done in the pan; liquid colors are best; trouble will be saved if used in the following order. Suppose Raspberry, Everton and Lemon taffies were wanted, make the Lemon taffy first, add saffron [Pg 23] just before the boil is ready, then the lemon, and pour out; make the Everton taffy next in the same way, add the butter before the lemon; then make the Raspberry. In this arrangement there is no necessity of steaming out the pan. Had the Raspberry taffy been made first, the pan would have to be cleaned out before the Lemon or Everton taffy could have been made, because it would have been red.

Measure the flavors in a graduated glass; wash out the glass frequently, or it will get rancid; weigh the acid and see that it is well ground; if it has become dry and lumpy, rub it down to a powder with a rolling pin or heavy bottle on a sheet of paper before using. In using fruit essences a little powdered tartaric acid throws up the flavor, half the essences will have a better effect. Put the acid on the boil after it has been poured on the slab in a little heap, and pour the essence over it, then thoroughly incorporate the whole.

Use the best oil for the slab with a clean flannel cloth; keep the cloth in a saucer, if it lies about it falls on the floor and picks up dirt and carries it to the pouring plate. When it gets hard or gritty burn it at once and get a new one, or it may be used by mistake and make a mess. We have seen the beauty of a boil spoilt scores of times by using dirty rags and rancid oil. A sugar boiler cannot be too careful in these little details, the success of his work largely depends upon it. It is easy to inaugurate a good system, and much more comfortable to work to it than a slovenly "what shall I do [Pg 24] next" sort of a method. Know where to find and put your hand on everything; when the boil is hot there is no time to look for what you require. "A place for everything and everything in its place" should be a practical feature in every boiling shop.

STICKY CANDIES.

Perhaps there is nothing more annoying to the trade than sticky boiled sugars. All clear goods when exposed to the atmosphere will turn damp, especially in wet weather. It is a question of degree, some slightly and some will run almost to syrup; it is impossible to obviate the former but the latter can be prevented. Great care should be used in adding the lowering, whether cream of tartar or glucose, too much of either will cause the goods to run immediately after they are turned out. Weak or inferior sugars, or not sufficient boiling, has also this effect. We know of no reliable agent which will altogether prevent this result but we do know that a careful arrangement of the different proportions, using good sugar and well boiling greatly mitigate, if not altogether prevent the grievance. Goods intended for exposure should contain just sufficient lowering to prevent the boil from growing grainy and boiled right up to the standard. Of course different sugars will carry more or less lowering, but this can be easily tested by the workman. A few experiments will determine the exact quantity for each boil. There is no excuse for drops sticking in bottles when corked, [Pg 25] this should not occur, if it does, the fault is in the making; the water has a great deal to do with causing the candies to be sticky. The writer has experienced this in several country places, where the only supply of this indispensable ingredient was drawn from the artesian wells. To look at it, it was all that could be desired—a beautiful, cold, clear and wholesome beverage. Of its chemical constituents I do not pretend to give an opinion, but the drops and other clear boils for which it was used got damp directly after they were exposed, and would have run to a syrup had they not been covered up. The goods keep all right in bottles, but it is very annoying, not to speak of the injury and loss to a business, when this is the position with regard to the water supply. The only remedy we could suggest, and which was very successful, was powdered borax. We used this in the proportion of a teaspoonful to every 14 lbs. of sugar adding it just as the sugar began to boil. Borax has been found useful with any water when making goods to be exposed in the window or on the counters, such as taffies, rocks and clear boiled sugars generally. Where the supply of water, as in most large towns is suitable, given good sugar, cream of tartar or glucose, in proper proportions, and careful boiling up to the standard, the addition of borax is unnecessary and should only be resorted to under special circumstances.

PLAIN TAFFY.

14 lbs. White Sugar.
2 quarts Water.
½ ounce Cream Tartar.

[Pg 26]
Process. —This is an easy and capital recipe to begin with. The process is practically the same as for all other clear goods, but the ingredients being fewer there is little chance of their getting complicated. With a thermometer it is hardly possible to make a mistake, besides it will make the instruction more intelligible: should he not possess this appliance, we must ask that the instructions "How to boil sugar" should be committed to memory, as it would be tedious and a great waste of time and space to keep explaining how to tell the different degrees through which the sugar passes before it comes to the point required for the different goods given in this book. For this and other reasons I will assume the learner to be working with one.

Put the sugar and water in a clean pan, place it on the fire and stir it occasionally till melted; when it comes to the boil add the cream of tartar and put a lid on the pan; allow it to boil in this way for ten minutes, remove the lid and immerse the bottom part of the thermometer in the boiling liquid and allow it to remain in this position until it records 310 degrees, then quickly take out the thermometer, lift off the pan and pour contents into frames, tins, or on a pouring slab, which have been previously oiled. If on a pouring slab, mark the boil into bars or squares, while warm, with a knife or taffy cutter: when quite cold it is ready for sale.

LEMON TAFFY.

14 lbs. White Sugar.
½ ounce Cream Tartar.
Saffron Coloring.
2 quarts Water.
Lemon Flavoring.

[Pg 27]
Process. —Proceed as directed for plain taffy. When the sugar reaches 305 degrees, add a few drops of saffron color; when it reaches 310 degrees, add a few drops of oil of lemon and pour out immediately into frames or tins; or if on pouring slab, mark out into bars or squares before it gets cold. The pouring slab should be level so that the sheet should be all the same thickness.

BUTTER SCOTCH.

8 lbs. White Sugar.
1 lb. Fresh Butter.
Lemon Flavoring.
¼ oz. Cream of Tartar.
1 quart Water.

Process. —Melt the sugar in the water by an occasional stir when the pan is on the fire, then add the cream of tartar and boil up to 300, lift the pan on to the side of the furnace and add butter in small pieces broken off by the hand; slip the pan on the fire again, adding the lemon flavoring; let it boil through so that all the butter is boiled in then pour into frames; when partly cold mark with cutter into small squares; when cold divide the squares; wrap each in wax-paper; sold generally in one cent packages.

N.B.—There is good butter scotch and better butter scotch, but no bad butter scotch; this quality may be improved by the addition of a large proportion of butter: some makers would put 2 lbs. or even 3 lbs. to this quantity, but that would be regulated by the class of trade and the size squares. These frames are made to hold 144 squares; a boil this size will make each square [Pg 28] weigh about 1 oz., but any weight of square may be arranged by the adding or deducting from the boil.

EVERTON TAFFY.

12 lbs. White Sugar.
2 lbs. Dark Sugar.
2 lbs. Fresh Butter.
½ oz. Cream of Tartar.
2 quarts Water.
Lemon Flavoring.

Process. —Melt the sugar in the water, add the cream of tartar and boil the whole to the degree of 300; lift the pan on the side of the fire put in the butter in small pieces, place the pan again on the fire and let it boil through; add the lemon and give it time to mix in, then pour out contents into frame, or on pouring plate to cut up into bars. Everton taffy and butter scotch are similar, except in color; same remarks as to quality will apply in both cases; if the fire is very fierce, do not put the pan down flat on it after adding butter; nurse it gently to prevent burning; little fresh coke shaken over the fire would assist.

RASPBERRY TAFFY.

14 lbs. White Sugar.
½ oz. Cream of Tartar.
Raspberry Flavor.
2 quarts Water.
Brilliant Rose.

Process. —Bring the sugar and water to a boil, add the cream of tartar, put on the lid for ten minutes, then uncover and immerse the thermometer; continue to boil to 300; tinge a bright red with liquid, brilliant rose; add raspberry essence; pour out on frame or pouring plate and mark into bars or squares of convenient [Pg 29] size; when cold the taffy is ready for packing and sale.

FIG TAFFY.

10 lbs Good Yellow Sugar.
2 lbs. Glucose.
3 lbs Figs Chopped Fine.
3 pints Water.

Process. —Boil the sugar, water and glucose to a weak crack, 295; lift the pan partly off the fire, putting a piece of iron under it to prevent it burning; add the figs, gently letting the whole thoroughly boil through and mix; pour in oiled tins or on slab, and mark into squares. When adding the figs let them drop through the fingers, not in a heap.

WALNUT TAFFY.

5 lbs. Brown Sugar.
5 lbs. Crystal Sugar.
2½ lbs. Glucose.
3 lbs. Walnuts.
2 quarts Water.
Lemon Flavoring.

Process. —Shell the walnuts, peel off the skin chop very fine. Boil the glucose, sugar and water as before directed to the degree of weak crack, 300. Lift the pan a little from the fire; add the prepared nuts by letting them run through the finger gently; let the whole boil through, then add a few drops of the oil of lemon; when thoroughly mixed in, pour out the boil and mark into bars before too cold. The flavor is improved by roasting the walnuts a little before putting in the boil.

[Pg 30]

PEANUT CANDY.

Boil to the crack, 1 quart best New Orleans Molasses, 1 lb. glucose and 1 quart water.

Prepare the meats by removing the thin reddish skin in which they are enveloped and fill a tray to about the depth of an inch. Pour over them the hot candy prepared as directed, stirring the meats till each one is covered. A little less candy should be used than will suffice to entirely cover the meats, though each separate one should be covered, the object being to use just enough of the candy to cause the meats to adhere firmly together, thus forming a large cake, which when nearly cold may be divided into squares or bars with a sharp knife.

Almonds and other nuts may be used in the same manner above described.

BARCELONA TAFFY.

5 lbs. Brown Sugar.
5 lbs. Crystal Sugar.
3 lbs. Barcelona Nuts.
2 lbs. Glucose.
2 quarts Water.
Lemon Flavoring.

Prepare the nuts by chopping them fine, boil the sugar, glucose and water to the degree 300. Remove the pan a little from the fire add the nuts carefully; when thoroughly boiled through and amalgamated, add a few drops of lemon and pour out contents into frame or on pouring plate and mark into bars.

COCOANUT TAFFY.

6 lbs. Granulated Sugar.
2 lbs. Desiccated Cocoanut Unsweetened.
4 lbs. Brown Sugar.
2 lbs. Glucose.
3 pints Water.
Lemon Flavoring.

[Pg 31]

Process. —Melt the sugars in the water, bring it to the boil, add the glucose and continue to boil to the degree 300; lift the pan a little way from the fire; let the desiccated cocoanut run gently in the boil; continue to boil until the lot is well mixed through; add a few drops of oil of lemon and pour out in frames; use the lemon cautiously, too much spoils the flavor.

Fig. 14.
Cocoanut Slicer and Shredder. IM GRATER.
Pat. Aug. 30, 1887.

No. 2 we claim to be the best Hand Made Machine in the Market. It is easily adjusted for cutting, slicing or grating, the several plates requiring but a moment to adjust to the shaft. It is the only machine having an outside adjustment.

No. 2 Machine, Slicer and Shredder	$20 00
Grater for same	3 00

[Pg 32]

COCOANUT TAFFY OR STICK JAW.

6 lbs. Granulated Sugar.
4 lbs. Brown sugar.
3 pints Water.
2 lbs. Glucose.
4 Large Cocoanuts Sliced.

Process. —Boil to crack 310 by the thermometer, the sugar, glucose and water; have the cocoanut freshly peeled and sliced ready; raise the pan two or three inches from the fire; slide in the nut, stirring gently with spatula to keep them off the bottom till well boiled through, then pour out in tins or frames.

N.B.—Stir gently only the one way or you may grain the boil.

Fig. 13.
Citron and Orange Peel Slicing Machin
This is a useful Machine for Slicing Pee
tops of Maderia Cakes, etc.

It is also made double-action i.e.—
Knives, the latter being used to shred o[r]
Price, $13 00
[Pg 33]

EGGS AND BACON.

10 lbs. White Sugar.
2½ lbs. Glucose.
3 pints Water.
1 lb. Nonpareils.
1 Cocoanut.
Brilliant Rose Coloring.

Process. —Cut a large cocoanut into slices, dry them and lay them on the pouring plate in rows about half an inch apart; sprinkle between them thickly some nonpareil of various colors (hundreds and thousands). Boil to crack the sugar, glucose and water; tinge with brilliant rose, and carefully and evenly pour the contents over the pouring plate, disturbing the nut and nonpareil as little as possible. A good plan is to have a small shallow ladle with an open spout, into which pour a little of the boil, run over the plate a small stream from the ladle first, this will bind the nut, etc., and keep them in their places while the bulk is being poured out.

ALMOND HARDBAKE.

10 lbs. Good Brown Sugar.
2 lbs. Glucose.
Lemon Flavoring if desired.
3 lbs. Almonds.
3 pints water.

Process. —Split with a sharp knife the almonds, lay them face downwards on an oiled plate, cover the plate as closely as possible; boil the glucose, sugar and water to the crack 305; remove the pan from the fire, and pour the contents carefully and evenly over the almonds; the addition of a little lemon or almond flavoring will improve it.

N.B.—See remarks re-ladle in previous recipe.
[Pg 34]

ALMOND ROCK.

10 lbs. Brown Sugar.
2 lbs. Glucose.
6 lbs. Sweet Almonds.
3 pints water.

Process. —Clean your almonds by blowing out all the dust and grit, pick out the shells, dissolve the sugar water and glucose; boil the lot up to crack; pour the contents on oiled plate. Sprinkle the almond all over the boil, shake over the lot a few drops of oil of lemon; turn up the edges first, then the whole boil; mix and knead it like dough until all the almonds are well mixed in; no time must be lost in this process or the sugar will get too hard; when firm make a long roll of the entire boil, place it on a hard wood board, and cut it up into thin slices; it will have to be kept in shape while cutting, by turning over and pressing the sides as it becomes flat; a special large sharp knife is used for this purpose. A smaller boil than the above had better be tried by beginners, say half the quantity. This can be done by halving the ingredients. Needless to state these remarks apply to other recipes.

FRENCH ALMOND ROCK.

12 lbs. White Sugar.
3 lbs. Glucose.
6 lbs. Sweet Blanched Almonds.
4 pints water.

Process. —Boil the sugar, water and glucose in the usual way to the degree of weak crack, 305 by the thermometer, then ease the pan a little way off the fire, and let the almonds gently slide into the mass. Use the spatula a little just to [Pg 35] keep the almonds from sticking to the bottom, stirring lightly only the one way, then watch the boil carefully till it turns a light golden color; lift off the pan and pour the contents into the frames. The almond will come to the top better in tins than in pouring plates.

Of course a better quality is made by adding more almonds, or vice versa. The almond after being blanched should be spread on a tin and dried, either on the stove top or in the oven.

RASPBERRY CANDY.

12 lbs. White Sugar.
3 lbs. Raspberry Jam.
2 quarts water.
Brilliant Rose Coloring.

Process. —Melt the sugar in water, and boil to ball 250; add the raspberry jam, and stir it well in; remove the pan from the fire, add sufficient coloring to make bright raspberry; rub part of the mixture with spatula against side of pan until it changes a heavy opaque, then stir the whole mass until uniform. Pour the contents carefully on a slab, covered with greased paper; make the sheet about ½ inch thick, mark into bars with a sharp knife, and break up when cold.

APRICOT CANDY.

6 lbs. White Sugar.
2 lbs. Apricot Jam or Pulp.
2 pints water.
Saffron Coloring.

Process. —Melt the sugar in the water and boil to ball, 250, add the jam or pulp. Stir well until thoroughly mixed in, remove the pan, rub part of the contents [Pg 36] against the side of the pan with spatula until cloudy and opaque; color with saffron a bright yellow, then stir the whole together until uniform cloudy; pour out in frames or on slab covered with oiled paper. A pinch of tartaric acid would improve the flavor, but often prevent candying, unless in the hands of an expert. In any case the acid should be added in a fine powder after the whole has been thoroughly grained. A pallette knife is a very useful knife for rubbing the sugar against the sides of the pan.

BROWN COCOANUT CANDY.

14 lbs. Brown Sugar.
6 large Cocoanuts Sliced.
3 pints water.

Process. —Melt the sugar in the water, and boil to degree of ball, then add the sliced cocoanut, stir them in remove the pan from the fire and rub the sugar against the side of the pan until it becomes cloudy stir the whole together until the whole becomes cloudy and thick; turn out the batch into tins or on slabs; mark with a sharp knife into squares or bars. When cold break it up at marks. Prepare the cocoanuts by cutting them up into thin slices with a spokeshave or machine. The brown skin is seldom skinned off for this dark candy.

WHITE COCOANUT CANDY.

14 lbs. White Sugar.
6 Large Cocoanuts Peeled and Sliced.
3 pints Water.

Process. —Peel off all the brown skin from the nuts with a sharp knife; wash them and cut into thin slices. [Pg 37] Melt the sugar in the water and boil to ball 250, add the sliced nuts, keeping the boil well stirred. When thoroughly mixed, remove the pan from the fire and commence to grain with pallette knife or spatula until the whole mass turns an opaque white. Now turn out the batch into frames, or on the slab, which has been covered with paper; mark into convenient sized bars, break up when set hard.

CHOCOLATE COCOANUT CANDY.

10 lbs. Brown Sugar.
1 lb. Pure Block Cocoa.
4 Cocoanuts shredded.
3 pints water.

Process. —When cracking the nuts, do so over a basin and save all the milk: peel all brown skin off and cut the nut into fine shreds with machine; dissolve the sugar in the pan with the water and cocoanut milk, boil up to ball, remove the pan a little off the fire, then add the nut together with the pure block cocoa, stir the whole together, grain on side of pan as before directed. Stir the whole well up and turn out into frames or on pouring plates.

N.B.—The pure cocoa should have been previously melted in a saucepan or chopped up in small pieces. In the latter case there is less waste, and the heat of the sugar would soon melt it.

FRUIT CANDY.

7 lbs. White or Brown Sugar.
1 lb. Currants cleaned and dried.
½ lb. Sultanas.
½ lb. Sweet Almonds.
2 pints water.
Saffron Coloring.
[Pg 38]

Process. —Mix together the fruits, which should have been freed from grit and dust; boil the sugar and water to the degree of ball, 250; remove the pan from the fire; gently grain the boil by rubbing a little of the syrup against the side of the pan until cloudy, then slide in the fruit and stir the whole together, adding a little saffron to color a bright yellow. See that the mass has changed to an opaque, then turn the lot out into frames or on a pouring slab.

CANDIES, VARIOUS.

Fruits green, dried or preserved, almonds and nuts of almost every description, as well as flavors and colors of a pleasant taste and pretty hue may be used in making candies. The process is exactly the same: the ingredients can be arranged to suit the fancy of the maker and the palate of his customers. The field to select variety from seems inexhaustible, so that new goods of this class should be introduced ad. lib. No good purpose could be served by giving a procession of these simple instructions, when with little thought and judgment anyone could invent a new candy for themselves. It might be as well to add that a little glucose or cream of tartar added will make the candies softer, and may be used, if preferred, in each formula in the proportion of 2 lbs. of glucose or a teaspoonful of cream tartar to every 10 lbs. of sugar.

[Pg 39]
ROLLER PATTERNS.

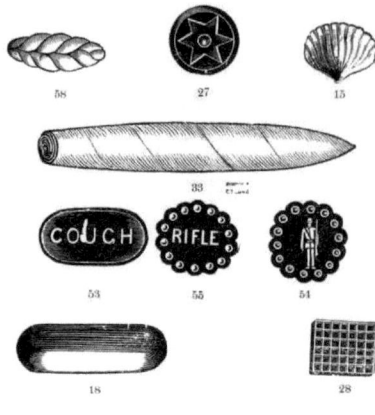

No.		To lb.
1	Tom Thumb Drop	1000
2	Currant Drop	840
3	Acid Drop	500
4	Sour Ball	250
5	Sour Ball	180
6	Fish	200
7	Fish	150
8	Fish	120
9	Fish	60
10	Fish	40
11	Strawberry	200
12	Raspberry	200
15	Shell	200
16	Motto Lump	200
17	Motto Lump	120
18	Motto Lump	80
27	Seal Cough	200
28	Waffle	180
33	Cigar	35
37	Heart and Hand	100
38	Acorn	209
42	Batton	200
53	Cough	120
54	Polka	200
55	Rifle	150
58	Twist Loaf	200

[Pg 40]

BARLEY SUGAR DROPS.

14 lbs. White Sugar.
3 lbs. Glucose.
4 pints water.
¼ oz. Oil Lemon.
Saffron Coloring.

Process. —Put the sugar and water in a pan, place it on the fire, giving it an occasional stir until the sugar is dissolved, then add the glucose, or ¼ oz. cream of tartar—either will do, but do not use both—place the cover on the pan and let it boil for ten minutes or so, (the cover is put on to steam the sides of the pan and keep it clean and free from granulation); take off the cover and put in the thermometer, immersing the bottom part in the boiling liquid. Let the whole boil until it reaches the degree of crack, 300; tinge with saffron, then pour the contents on pouring plate, which has been previously oiled; sprinkle a few drops of oil of lemon over it, turn the edges as it begins to cool: then turn it over, knead it up as soon as you can handle it: if it is on a cool slab you must be pretty smart or it will get too hard. As soon as it gets stiff enough cut off small convenient pieces and pass through the barley sugar machine; when cool break up, give them a good shake in a rough sieve to free them from any machine scraps; the drops are then ready for bottling. Powdered sugar is not usually mixed with these drops.

PEAR DROPS.

14 lbs. White Sugar.
3 lbs Glucose.
¼ oz. Essence of Pear.
1 oz. Tartaric Acid.
2 quarts water.
Paste, Red Color.

[Pg 41]

Process. —Dissolve the sugar in the water, add the glucose, and bring the whole to the degree of crack, pour the contents on the slab, rub in a little red paste color in one corner of the boil to color light pink, turn up the edges, add the powdered acid in a little heap, pour over the acid the pear essence and thoroughly mix through the entire mass by kneading: when the batch is stiff enough cut off in small pieces and pass through the pear drop rollers; when cold sift and mix some icing sugar amongst them, and bottle.

RASPBERRY DROPS.

14 lbs. White Sugar.
2 quarts water.
3 lbs. Glucose.
½ oz. Essence of Raspberry.
1 oz. Tartaric.
Coloring, Brilliant Rose.

Process. —Melt the sugar in the water, add the glucose and boil the whole up to crack; pour out the boil on a cold slab, rub in a little of the cherry paste to color, turn up the edges, put in the powdered acid in a little heap, pour over the acid the raspberry flavoring and knead up the batch till thoroughly mixed and fit for the machine. Cut off in pieces and pass through the raspberry rollers; sift, dust and bottle when cold.

ALMOND TABLETS.

14 lbs. Brown Sugar.
3 lbs Glucose.
Lemon Flavoring.
2 lbs. Almonds, Chopped.
4 pints water.

Process. —Boil the sugar, glucose and water, as directed, to the degree of crack; pour the boil on oiled [Pg 42] plate, sprinkle the almond over it with a few drops of oil of lemon, knead the whole together till stiff, cut off small pieces and pass through tablet rollers.

PINE APPLE DROPS.

14 lbs. White Sugar.
3 lbs. Glucose.
4 pints water.
1 oz. Tartaric Acid.
Saffron Coloring.
¼ oz. Essence Pine Apple.

Process. —Boil the sugar, glucose and water, as before directed, to the degree of crack 310; add to the boil saffron paste after it has been poured on the slab: when on the slab put in the acid and essence of pineapple; knead the whole together; when stiff enough, cut off in pieces and pass through the pineapple roll.

COCOANUT TABLETS.

14 lbs. White Sugar.
3 lbs. Glucose.
1 lb. Desiccated Cocoanut.
4 pints water.

Process. —Boil the sugar, water and glucose to the degree of crack; pour on slab and sprinkle the desiccated cocoanut over the boil, flavor with lemon, mix up and pass through tablet rollers.

ACID DROPS AND TABLETS.

14 lbs. Best White Sugar.
¾ oz. Cream of Tartar.
Lemon Flavoring.
4 pints water.
4 oz. Tartaric Acid.

Process. —Put the sugar and water in clean bright pan and bring to the boil, add cream of tartar, place the lid on the pan and boil for ten minutes: remove the [Pg 43] cover and put in thermometer, boiling on a sharp fire to the degree of crack: pour out at once on clean, greased slab: when cool enough, turn up at the edges and fold the boil over, then add the acid which has been finely powdered, together with a few drops of lemon; knead up the whole until stiff and pass through drop or tablet rollers; break up when cold, and dust with powdered sugar, weigh and bottle.

N.B.—We mean the term "white sugar" to include loaf, dutch crush, granulated or crystal; any of these of good quality will answer the purpose.

BROWN COUGH DROPS.

14 lbs. Brown Sugar.
3 lbs. Glucose.
3 oz. Acid Tartaric.
½ oz. Oil Aniseed.
¼ oz. Oil Cloves.
¼ oz. Oil Peppermint.
2 oz. Herb Horehound.
5 pints Water.

Process. —First boil the herb horehound in the water ten minutes, then strain; add the liquor to the sugar and the glucose, and boil as for other drops to crack 310; pour on oiled slab; turn up the edges and fold in the boil, then put the tartaric acid in a little heap on the boil, and pour over it the aniseed, clove and peppermint, knead up the whole, thoroughly mixing the flavors until stiff enough to pass through machine cough drop rollers.

N.B.—The brown sugar should be of good boiling quality.

[Pg 44]

LIGHT COUGH DROPS.

14 lbs. White Sugar.
3 lbs. Glucose.
3 oz. Acid Tartaric.
½ oz. Cough Drop Essence.
½ oz. Oil Aniseed.
4 pints Water.

Process. —Boil the sugar, glucose and water as before directed to the degree of crack, 310; pour on greased slab; first turn up boil, then add powdered acid, cough drop essence and oil of aniseed; mix thoroughly until ready for machine, and pass through cough drop rollers; break up, sift, and dust with powdered sugar.

N.B.—We have almost said enough about plain machine drops; they are all practically made alike, the color, flavor and shape alone differing. See *our* list for *colors* and *flavors, candy machines* and *rollers.*

TAR COUGH DROPS.

1 oz. Dried Rose Leaves boil in 1 gallon water to half a gallon, strain and mix with 10 pounds Sugar, 21 pounds Glucose and 1 oz. strained Tar, boil to the crack and finish as for other drops.

IMITATION CHOCOLATE STICKS.

8 lbs. White Sugar.
2 lbs. Glucose.
Vanilla Flavoring.
3 pints Water.
1 oz. Tartaric Acid.

Process. —Place the pan containing the sugar and water on the fire, stir in the glucose and bring the lot to the degree of weak crack, 300; pour on the slab, turn up the edges, fold over the boil, and add the acid and vanilla; when thoroughly mixed and stiff enough [Pg 45] to handle, then pull over the hook until glossy white: remove it to the slab, and roll into rods about half an inch thick; when cold snip off into short equal lengths and dip them into melted chocolate paste, composed of ½ lb. pure block cocoa, ½ lb. ground sugar and 3 oz. lard or cocoa butter (no water). Melt these ingredients in a vessel by standing it on the hot furnace plate (not too near the fire) stir until all is dissolved and incorporated, then dip sticks in this mixture singly, taking them out immediately and laying them on wire frames to dry.

CHOCOLATE COCOANUT STICKS.

8 lbs. White Sugar.
2 lbs. Glucose.
Desiccated Cocoanut.
3 pints Water.
4 oz. Pure Cocoanut.

Process. —Boil the sugar, water and glucose as directed to degree of weak crack, 300; pour on oiled slab: cut off one third for pulling; add to the other two-thirds the pure cocoa and mix it in; pull the smaller piece over the hook until white and glossy; spread out the solid sugar and lay the pulled in the centre casing it round evenly then roll into sticks 1 inch thick; when cold, snip off into lengths make a thin solution of gum or gelatine, wet the surface of each stick, and roll in desiccated cocoa nut; when dry they are ready for sale.

ACID STICKS.

Clear white.
10 lbs. White Sugar.
2 oz. Tartaric Acid.
Lemon Flavoring.
½ oz. Cream of Tartar.
3 pints water.

[Pg 46]

Process. —Put the sugar and water in a clean bright pan, add the cream of tartar and boil up sharply to a weak crack, 300; pour the batch on oiled slab; turn in the edges, fold the boil over, then put in powdered acid with a few drops of lemon; knead the whole together, working one end down to a point; draw it out the required thickness, the full length of the plate, cut it off, then do another length likewise, repeating the operation until the boil is worked up; keep the first piece in shape by occasionally rolling them while the remainder of the boil is being pulled out and shaped. When the boil is finished, and the sticks cold, snip them off in lengths with scissors. An assistant is very useful to keep the sticks in motion while the boil is being worked up or they may become flat.

PEPPERMINT STICKS.

Dark brown with light stripes.
8 lbs. Brown Sugar.
2 lbs. Glucose.
3 pints Water.
Peppermint Flavoring.

Process. —Bring the sugar, glucose and water to the degree of crack in the usual way; pour the batch on the slab; work in the flavors; cut off a piece about 1½ pounds from the boil and pull it over hook until light and satiny, then roll the pulled sugar out into a long stick, cut it into six pieces of equal length and lay them on the solid boil longways and equal distances apart, then roll the boil into shape, bring down one end to a point; pull out into convenient lengths, twisting [Pg 47] them so that the stripes form a pretty spiral round the stick.

N.B.—For the stripes in this case, white sugar is often used and looks much better, but to do so two pans are necessary, one may be a small saucepan to boil two pounds. The white sugar is boiled separately in the ordinary way, otherwise, process, would be exactly as described.

LEMON STICKS.

Pulled yellow centre with yellow case.
8 lbs. White Sugar.
2 lbs Glucose.
Yellow Paste Color.
3 pints Water.
Lemon Essence.

Process. —Boil the sugar, glucose and water to a weak crack; pour the batch on oiled slab; work in color and flavor; cut off one-third and pull over the hook until of a bright yellow satiny appearance; remove it from the hook; spread out the plain sugar and lay the pulled in the centre; case it nicely all round with solid, then commence to roll; bring one end down to required thickness; pull out into sticks as long as convenient, when cold snip into lengths required.

ORANGE STICKS.

Pulled white body with one broad red and two narrow orange stripes.

8 lbs. White Sugar.
2 lbs. Glucose.
3 pints Water.
Red Coloring.
Oil of Orange.
Tartaric Acid.

[Pg 48]

Process. —Boil the sugar, glucose and water to the weak crack, 300; pour batch on slab; cut off about one-third of the boil; divide this into two pieces; color one-part a deep red and the other a deep orange; mix in the colors quickly and stand them aside on a piece of wood in a warm place till wanted; now put the acid and flavoring into the larger portion of the boil and pull over the hook until white and spongey; remove it to the slab, then take the piece of red sugar and draw it out about 18 inches long and 2½ inches wide; lay it down the centre of the pulled sugar, then take the piece of orange sugar and pull it out about 3 feet, half the thickness of the red, cut in two and place one on each side of the red, about two inches from it, roll, twist and pull out the recognized thickness; when cold, snip in lengths.

CINNAMON STICKS.

Clear pink body with four narrow white stripes.

6 lbs. White Sugar.
2 lbs. Glucose.
Cinnamon Flavor.
3 pints water.
Cherry Paste Color.

Process. —Bring the sugar, glucose and water to the crack and pour out; cut off piece and pull it white: color the body light pink, add the flavor, prepare the four stripes as before directed, lay them on the clear sugar, equal distance apart, roll out in lengths and snip off when cold.

[Pg 49]

CLOVE STICKS.

Almost transparent with a tinge of red, striped with white and red stripes alternately.

8 lbs. Sugar.
2 lbs. Glucose.
3 pints water.
Cherry Paste Color.
Oil of Cloves.

Process. —Boil the sugar, glucose and water to 300; pour on the oiled slab; cut off small portion, divide it into two, color one deep red, pull both stripes and lay them alternately on the solid sugar, form the boil into a roll, bring down one end, usually the left end, to a point; pull out in long lengths and twist; when cold snip with scissors to size.

RASPBERRY STICKS.

Pulled white centre, cased with red and striped with six narrow white stripes.

8 lbs. White Sugar
2 lbs. Glucose.
3 pints water.
Cherry Red Paste Color.
Raspberry Essence.

Process. —Boil the sugar, glucose and water to crack 300; pour the batch on plate; cut in half and color one half red, then flavor both halves with essence, (raspberry and a little tartaric acid); pull one half over the hook and cut off one third of it and lay it aside; put the other two thirds in the centre of the red solid sugar and case it around; now lay the remaining piece of pulled sugar in six lengths of equal thickness and distances apart on the top of the cased boil; roll out the ball to the required thickness, twist and snip off into lengths when cold.

[Pg 50]

TWISTED BARLEY SUGAR STICKS.

Hand Made.

8 lbs. White Sugar.
2 lbs. Glucose.
3 pints water.
Lemon Flavoring.
Saffron Color.

Process. —Put the sugar and water in a clear, bright pan and bring to a boil, then add the glucose: put on the lid for five minutes, continue boiling in the usual way till it reaches crack 300; now add sufficient coloring to tinge a golden color and pour the boil carefully over the smooth slab, so that the sheet of sugar will not be more than the eighth of an inch thick. When the sheet has partly set, cut it into strips one inch wide and the whole length of the sheet with scissors. Let an assistant take charge of the strips and twist them by taking hold of an end in each hand and turn them in opposite directions, forming a spiral column; when cold snip the required lengths and carefully weigh and bottle. To make these goods the operators must be very quick in their movements. The slab must be warm on which the sugar is poured, as the thin sticks cool so fast and get brittle.

PEPPERMINT BULL'S EYES.

For cornered drops cut at angles, black with white stripes.

8 lbs. Brown Sugar.
2 lbs Glucose.
3 pints water.
Peppermint Flavor.

Process. —The process is exactly the same as for peppermint stick, viz; boil the sugar water and glucose [Pg 51] to weak crack, 300; pour the boil on oiled plate, flavor with peppermint and work well up; in a smaller pan have two pounds of white sugar, with the usual proportion of cream of tartar and water boiled to the same degree; pull this over the hook until white and porous; remove it to the plate and work it down into lengths about one inch thick; lay them longways on the solid boil, equal distances apart; make the whole boil into a thick roll, bringing one end down to a point; draw off as for one cent sticks, but thicker; then with scissors snip them off in pieces about an inch long. Hold the scissors in the right hand, the sugar in the left; every time you make a clip turn the sugar half way round, so that the corners of each cushion will be at opposite angles.

BULL'S EYES, (Various.)

The formula given for the different kinds of sugar sticks will answer for the variety of bull's eyes. The process and ingredients are precisely alike. The sticks may or may not be drawn out a little thicker, according to the size of drop required. Cream of tartar may be substituted for glucose in all recipes given for boiled goods. The sugar is not boiled quite so high for hand goods or pulled sugar as it is for machine drops; being a little lower it works better, keeps longer pliable, and is less brittle when cold.

ROUND BALLS.

8 lbs. Sugar.
2 lbs. Glucose.
Color.
3 pints water.
Flavor.

[Pg 52]

Process. —Boil the sugar, water and glucose in the usual way to weak crack, say 300; pour the boil on the slab, color and flavor to taste; work the batch up until stiffish, then roll the boil round, getting one end down to a point as directed for sticks, pull it off in lengths of about three feet and about one inch thick; cut in pieces with " Jackson Ball Cutter " and roll round with the hand. An expert assistant is necessary for this operation, as the balls must be shaped while hot and kept on the move till cold.

No.	Cuts	Balls	Diameter
1		8 balls,	1 1/8 inch diameter (wedge)
2		11 balls,	13-16 " "
3		9 balls,	1 inch " "

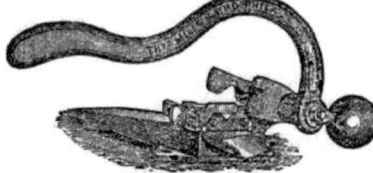

Fig. 210 a.

[Pg 53]

This general recipe will apply to all balls. For details of pulling, striping, casing and variety the reader is referred to the various processes given for sticks and bulls eyes. They are all made and finished in this way. For small sizes, pull out the lengths thinner; for large sizes, thicker.

To make the various striped balls nicely, requires practice and a good deal of it. No amount of book learning will teach those who are quite ignorant of sugar boiling; but at the same time if the reader has mastered the simpler process at the beginning of the book, he is quite capable of understanding this and working out his own ideas in this way; but hand-made balls should not be attempted until the learner feels confident he can manage a boil easily and quickly, because there is no time to think after the sugar is on the slab. The manipulation must now have been acquired to an extent so as to enable the operator to proceed as if by instinct.

ROSE BUDS.

8 lbs. White Sugar.
2 pounds glucose.
5 or 6 drops Otto of Roses.
3 pints water.
Cherry Paste Color.

Process. —Boil the sugar, glucose and water to the degree of crack 300, pour on oiled slab, cut off about one third for pulling, color the larger piece a deep red and flavor with otto of roses; pull the smaller piece over the hook till white; spread out the larger piece, [Pg 54] lay the pulled sugar in the middle, casing carefully round, pass through small acid drop rollers.

N.B.—Turn the boil on its edge every time you cut a piece for the machine, in order to keep the pulled sugar as near the centre as possible.

RIPE PEARS.

8 lbs Sugar.
2 lbs. Glucose.
3 pints water.
1 oz. Tartaric Acid.
Cherry Red.
Yellow Paste Color.
1/4 oz. Essence Pear.

Process. —Melt the sugar in the water, add the glucose and boil to 305; pour on slab, cut the batch into three equal parts, flavor with essence of pear, together with a little acid, color one part deep red and one deep yellow, pull the third portion over the hook and lay it between the yellow and red pieces so that one side will be yellow and the other bright red; cut off into convenient sizes and pass through large pear drop rollers. These goods are sold either plain or crystalized.

BOILED SUGAR TOYS.

See our stock of clear toy moulds, list of which is mailed on application. They may be had to turn out all kinds of figures, such as dogs, cats, elephants, etc. They are very popular among the children and sell well in certain districts, and show a handsome profit. The moulds are generally made in two parts; they must be well oiled; the sugar boiled as for drops. Fill [Pg 55] the moulds full, and just before the whole mass sets, pour as much of the sugar out as will run; this will leave only a thin coating which cling to the sides of the shapes and will easily come out when the mould is parted, then you have the figures complete but hollow. Boiled sugar whistles are made exactly the same way.

TO CRYSTALIZE BOILED SUGAR GOODS.

Several descriptions of boiled sugars are sold crystalized, which look very pretty and stand exposure to the atmosphere better. The process is very simple and may be done with little trouble. When the drops have been made and set, break them up and sift them well in a coarse sieve, now shake them over a pan which is boiling, so that they get damped by steam, and throw them in a heap of crystal sugar; mix them well up, so that the sugar adheres to the drops uniformly; now sift them out of the sugar again and they will dry in a few minutes and be ready for packing. Another method is, when the drops have been made and sifted, to have a thin solution of gum or gelatine and shake it over them and rub them all together till damp all over; now throw over them sufficient crystal sugar to coat them and mix them up; when dry sift again and pack.

N.B.—When being crystalized the goods should be warm, not hot, or they will candy. Large French pears should be crystalized by the latter process and [Pg 56] be almost cold during the operation; being bulky they retain the heat a long time, and therefore have a great tendency to grain.

IMITATION INDIAN CORN.

8 lbs. White Sugar.
2 lbs. Glucose.
Yellow Color.
3 pints Water.
Lemon Flavoring.

Process. —Boil the sugar, glucose and water to weak crack, 305; pour the boil on slab, flavor with lemon and color yellow; cut this boil in two and pull one-half over the hook; roll the pulled half out in lengths about the size of a corn pod; now put the plain yellow sugar through the Tom Thumb drop rollers, loosening the screws a little, and ease the pulled sugar with sheets from the machine; if done carefully, the result will be a good imitation of real Indian corn.

POPCORN BALLS.

Roast the corn berries over a smokeless fire in a corn popper (get our price for corn poppers); keep shaking until every berry has burst; boil sufficient sugar and water to the degree of feather, 245; add to each 7 lbs. syrup, four ounces of dissolved gum arabic; wet the popped corn in this syrup, and roll them in fine pulverized sugar until coated all over, then lay them aside; when dry repeat the coating process in the same manner until they have taken up the desired thickness of sugar. Weigh or measure sufficient coated berries, according to size of ball required, moisten them with [Pg 57] thin syrup, partly form the ball by hand, then put it in a pop corn ball press and press tightly into shape, then form into balls in the usual way with pop corn ball press.

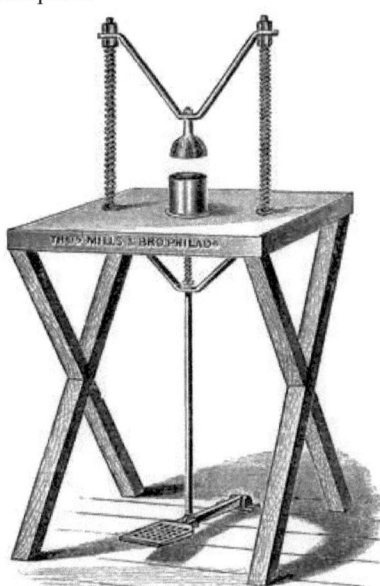

Fig. 208 a.

POPCORN BRICKS.

Process. —The corn berries are prepared as for balls; boil brown sugar in the proportion of 8 lbs. sugar and two pounds molasses to ball, 250; pour the syrup over the corn and thoroughly mix them; press them [Pg 58] immediately into oiled tins. The process should be done quickly and the seeds pressed as tightly together as possible; when cold they are ready for sale and may be cut to size with sharp knife.

POP CORN HAND BALL PRESS.

Fig. 209 a.

POP CORN CAKES.

Process. —Prepare the corn as for balls and pack them closely into strong square tins slightly oiled with olive oil of best quality; boil to crack, sufficient brown sugar and glucose for quantity required and pour the hot syrup over the pop corns, just enough to make them adhere. When cold cut them up with a sharp knife the size.

CORN POPPERS—Made Very Strong.

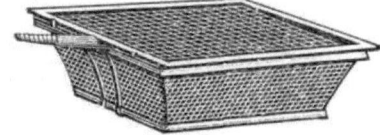

Fig. 523.

JAP NUGGETS NO. 1.

2 lbs. White Sugar.
4 lbs. Glucose.
4 lbs. Desiccated Cocoanut unsweetened.
Yellow Coloring.
1½ lbs. Farina.
2 pints Water.

[Pg 59]

Process.—Mix the ingredients in copper pan; boil on a slow fire to stiff ball, 250, stirring all the time; add coloring to fancy; when ready, pour carefully on an oiled plate, making the sheet about half an inch thick; when cold, dust with pulverized sugar and cut up with sharp knife to size.

N.B.—A few loose iron bars are useful to form a square on the pouring plate, in proportion to size of boil; that the exact thickness of sheet may be determined.

PATENT CANDY CUTTER.
For Cutting Caramels, Japanese Cocoan
 Cuts all thicknesses up to one inch, inches.
 Moving Bed of Machine is 32 inche pounds of Candy per day.
 One of the handiest and most useful a Price, $75 00
[Pg 60]

JAP NUGGETS NO. 2.
2 lbs. White Sugar.
4 lbs. Good Brown.
5 lbs. Desiccated Cocoanut.
7 lbs. Glucose.
2½ lbs. Farina.
3 pints Water.

Process.—Put the sugar, glucose and water in the pan; place it on a slow fire; stir in the cocoanut and farina and boil to stiff ball, 255, keeping it well stirred. Pour on an oiled slab, and cut up to size; when set, dust with powdered sugar. In large factories where this candy is made, machinery plays an important part. In fact the manipulation is practically all done by mechanism. There is the desiccator for preparing the cocoanuts, the steam pans, which are fitted with beaters revolving inside, fixed with chains and weights for lifting them out, so that the cans may be emptied and cleaned without trouble; also plates for rolling out sheets to size, and cutting machines which cut the nuggets any size, the machine being so arranged that by simply altering a pawl on a ratchet wheel the size of the nuggets is determined. Where this elaborate arrangement exists our formula would neither be desirable nor necessary, nor do we pretend to suggest or advise. However, many tons are made in the ordinary boiling shop with the usual appliances and conveniences, and it is to assist people thus situated is the principal object of this book.
[Pg 61]

JAP NUGGETS NO. 3.
4 lbs. Good Brown Sugar.
3½ lbs. Glucose.
3 pints Water.
4 lbs. Desiccated Cocoanut Unsweetened.
2 lbs. Farina.

Process.—As before, brown coloring should be used if required dark; it makes goods look richer; when the boil is cut up the nuggets should be thrown into pulverized sugar.

VANILLA NOUGAT (Common.)
12 lbs. White Sugar.
3 lbs. glucose.
½ oz. Essence Vanilla.
4 lbs. Sweet Almonds small.
3 pints water.

Process.—Put the sugar, glucose and water in a clean pan, place it on a sharp fire and stir until dissolved; then put on the cover and let it boil for five or six minutes; now remove the lid and continue to boil to soft ball degree; now pour the contents on a damp slab (one over which water has been sprinkled); when cool take a long flat spatula and work the sugar about until it becomes white and creamy; now add the almonds (which have been previously blanched and dried), together with the vanilla essence; keep working up the whole until of uniform consistency; now spread the mass on wafer paper in sheets one inch thick, cover the sheets with wafer paper, rolling the top smooth; when set cut into bars. Should the cream be a little thin add some icing sugar when mixing; if boiled properly this is not required. Most cheap Nougats now in the market are made more or less according to this formula, color and flavor differently for variety.
[Pg 62]

ICE CREAM CONFECTIONERY.
Boil 7 lbs. of loaf sugar with three pints of water: add a small teaspoonful of cream of tartar, allow it to boil for 10 minutes, then add one pound of fresh butter: it will then commence to froth up, and care must be taken that the pan is large enough, as the syrup will occupy twice the space than if there had been no butter added; boil this mixture to the degree of very weak crack, or 285 by the thermometer, at which point it is done; pour it on the slab, which has been of course previously greased. As soon as it begins to cool, turn it up and knead it until it gets stiff enough to pull over the hook. When on the hook pull it sharp till it gets white as snow. This white is usually flavored with vanilla or oil of lemon. It may be either pulled out in bars or left in the heap. It is very easily broken in small pieces for retail purposes. In the summer or hot weather keep this candy from the air, or it will be inclined to be sticky. This eats very rich and commands good sale at best prices.

RASPBERRY AND STRAWBERRY ICE CREAM CONFECTIONERY.
This is made exactly as the last with the addition of a little red color before the boil is poured out, or it may be colored on the slab; add a little essence of raspberry or strawberry and a pinch of tartaric acid just before pulling the boil. Color the raspberry a little deeper than the strawberry.
[Pg 63]

CHOCOLATE ICE CREAM.
To make chocolate ice cream, boil the same quantities as before precisely in the same way in every particular. When the sugar has been pulled out, work well into it ½ lb. powdered chocolate; knead this well up in order that the chocolate may be well mixed with the sugar. Put

in sufficient chocolate to give the boil a dark brown color, otherwise it would be too light when pulled.

VANILLA CARAMELS.

8 lbs. White Sugar.
2 lbs. Glucose.
1 lb. Fresh Butter.
2 Tins Condensed milk.
2 pints water.
Vanilla Flavoring.

Process. —Boil the sugar, glucose and water to the degree of ball 250; remove the pan a little from the fire, add the milk and butter, the latter cut into little pieces and well stir in with wooden spatula until the whole is thoroughly mixed, then gently bring the mass through the boil and pour out on greased slab, making the sheet about ½ inch thick; when set cut with caramel cutter, and when cold separate the squares and wrap in wax paper.

COCOANUT CARAMELS.

8 lbs. Sugar.
2 lbs. glucose.
1 lb. Fresh Butter.
1½ lbs. Desiccated Cocoanut, unsweetened.
2 Tins Condensed Milk.
2 pints water.

Process. —Melt the sugar in the water, add the glucose and boil up to ball 250; remove the pan to side, [Pg 64] then stir in the butter, milk and cocoanut, bring through the boil, pour on slab or in frames about ½ inch thick; when set mark with caramel cutter; when cold separate and wrap in wax paper.

CLADS PATTERN COCOANUT GRA
Extra Strong, Two Graters. Clamps to T

Fig. 21.

Citron and Cocoanut Cutter.
No. 1 Large Price, $1 20
A very handy and useful slicer. Durab

RASPBERRY CARAMELS.

8 lbs. Sugar.
2 lbs. glucose.
1 lb. Fresh Butter.
Brilliant Rose Color.
1 lb. Raspberry Pulp or Jam.
2 Tins Condensed milk.
2 pints water.

Process. —Boil the sugar, glucose and water to weak crack 250; remove the pan to side of fire, add [Pg 65] the milk, butter (cut small) and jam; stir the whole together, replacing the pan on the fire; add sufficient coloring; keep stirring all the time until the whole comes through the boil; pour out, mark with set, divide and wrap when cold.

WALNUT CARAMELS.

8 lbs. White Sugar.
1 lb. Shelled Walnuts broken small.
2 lbs. Glucose.
1 lb. Fresh Butter.
Saffron Coloring.
2 tins Condensed Milk.
2 pints Water.

Process. —As above, caramels require careful watching and a lot of stirring, the boil being liable to catch and flow over; fire must not be too fierce; when too hot put an iron under one side of the pan to keep it up a little from the fire; keep constantly on the stir after butter and flavoring ingredients are added.

CHOCOLATE CARAMELS.

8 lbs. Good Sugar.
½ lb. Pure Chocolate unsweetened.
2 lbs Glucose.
1 lb. Fresh Butter.
Vanilla Flavoring.
2 pints Water.
2 tins Condensed Milk.

Process. —When the sugar, glucose and water have been boiled to the degree of ball, 250, and the milk, butter and chocolate have all dissolved and incorporated, bring gently through the boil, then pour out on oiled slab or in frames; when set, mark deeply with caramel cutter; when cold, separate with sharp knife and wrap in wax paper. [Pg 66]

VANILLA CARAMELS NO. 1
Quality.

6 lbs. Sugar.
2 quarts Sweet Cream.
Essence of Vanilla.
15 lbs. Fresh Butter.
4 lbs. Glucose.

Process. —Put the sugar, glucose and cream in the pan; put it on a slow fire and stir constantly; let it boil to a stiff ball, then add the butter; keep stirring, when it has well boiled through, remove the pan from the fire; flavor with vanilla extract: pour out on oiled plate; mark when set with caramel cutter; when cold, divide with sharp knife and wrap each caramel in wax paper.

VANILLA CARAMELS, No. 2
Quality.

5 lbs. Sugar.
1 lb. Fresh Butter.
3 pints New Milk.
½ oz. Cream of Tartar.
2 pints water.
Vanilla Flavoring.

Process. —Boil the sugar, milk and water with the cream of tartar on a slow fire, stir all the time till it reaches a stiff ball, add the extract of vanilla and stir it gently; remove the pan from the fire and pour contents on oiled slab; mark deep with caramel cutter when set; when cold separate with sharp knife. These caramels should be cream color.

MAPLE CARAMELS.

By using pure maple, maple caramels may be made precisely as vanilla; the flavor of the maple sugar is sufficient without any artificial essence. These caramels will of course be dark. [Pg 67]

RASPBERRY AND STRAWBERRY CARAMELS.

These flavors may be used in either of the last two recipes—best quality according to the first, second quality as to the second. Walnut, cocoanut, etc., may be added for other flavors.

18 • The Candy Maker's Guide A Collection of Choice Recipes for Sugar Boiling • Fletcher Manufacturing Company

CHOCOLATE CARAMELS No. 1 Quality.

6 lbs. Best Sugar.
4 lbs. Glucose.
1½ lbs. Pure Chocolate, Unsweetened.
2 quarts Sweet Cream.
1½ lbs. Fresh Butter.

Process. —Put the sugar and cream in the pan, stir it well together, then add the glucose; let it boil to a stiff ball, ease the pan off the fire a little and put in the butter in little pieces, then the chocolate; keep stirring together; bring the mass through the boil, then add extract of vanilla; remove the pan and pour contents on oiled slab, making the sheet about ½ inch thick; mark deep with caramel cutter when set; divide with sharp knife when cold and wrap in paper.

CHOCOLATE CARAMEL, No. 2 Quality.

5 lbs. Sugar.
¾ lb. Fresh Butter.
1 quart of New Milk.
¾ lb. Pure Chocolate, Unsweetened.
½ oz. Cream of Tartar.

Process. —Melt the sugar in the milk, add the cream of tartar and boil to the degree of ball; ease the pan a little off the fire and stir in the butter and chocolate; bring the whole to a boil, add extract of vanilla, then remove the pan and pour contents on the slab; mark and separate as directed on last.

[Pg 68]

UNWRAPPED CARAMELS.

Caramels have usually been sold wrapped in wax paper. This is necessary when the goods are boiled very low and contain a large proportion of glucose. Like other caramels the ingredients vary, but the following will answer the purpose:—

7 lbs. White Sugar.
2 lbs. Glucose.
½ lb. Fresh Butter.
1 Tin Condensed Milk, or one quart Sweet Cream.
3 pints water.
Vanilla Flavoring.

Process. —Boil the sugar, glucose and water to weak crack 285; remove the pan from the fire, add the butter and milk, stir gently until dissolved, add the flavoring just before the stirring is finished, then pour contents on oiled slab; when cool enough cut with caramel cutter. If required crinkly on top; run over the sheet with a corded rolling pin just before cutting.

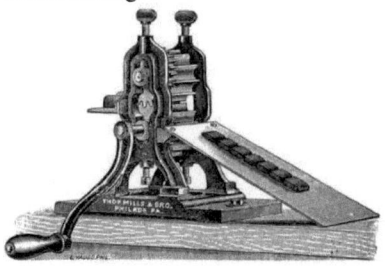

BUTTERCUP OR MIXED DROP MA(
This Machine is used for Cutting Butte
Has saw teeth for making crimped edge
Price, $19 00

[Pg 69]

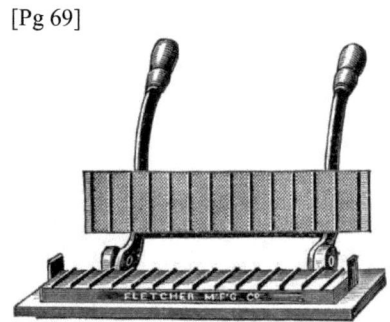

LATEST THING OUT.
NEW SATINETTE PRESS.
Buttercups and Satinettes will have a ve
Purchase one of our Machines and m
The Machine will pay for itself in a made goods.
Price $15.00

[Pg 70]
Cullums Patent Buttercup Cutter

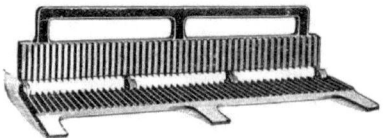

Fingers for Buttercup Cutters.

This is a Machine every Confectioner sl
No. 1 Machine is same as No. 2, but i and is the cheapest Machine ever put on
No. 2 Machine is 34 inches long, 4 glossy appearance. Cuts three times as f this Machine. Cut represents Lifter, the pieces of candy can be removed by one Machine with Teeth to form Buttercu
Price, $20 00

BUTTERCUPS.

These beautiful candies are very popular; they are pleasing both to the eye and the palate when they are well made, but they must be kept air tight or they will soon lose all their attractiveness and become a sticky mass, as they have a great tendency to "sweat." In order to prevent this as much as possible it is advisable to use a little borax in each boil. The process is [Pg 71] simple enough, but must be worked quickly, in fact the beauty depends upon the rapid manipulation of the sugar over the hook; keep the eye fixed on the color; as soon as it becomes a glossy satin with a close grain it is finished; lift it off the hook immediately and return to the slab for casing. Do not carry on the pulling operation until it becomes spongy, and be careful not to use too much color; the tints should be light and delicate when finished. Machines are made for cutting buttercups, price $6.00 and $14.00, each machine. Crimped edge machine, $20.00 each. *Get our price list.*

VANILLA BUTTERCUPS.

7 lbs. Best White Sugar.
2 lbs. Fondant Paste.
1 lb. Desiccated Cocoanut, fine.
Green color.
1 teaspoonful Cream of Tartar.
1 quart water.
Borax.

Process. —Put the sugar, water and cream of tartar in the boiling pan and boil up to crack 310 in the ordinary

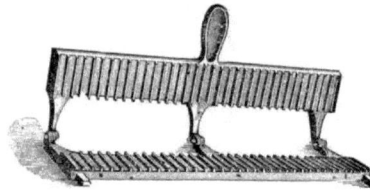

No. 1.

No. 2.

way; while the pan is on the fire, take the fondant paste and work into it the desiccated cocoanut, with a little essence of vanilla, and lay aside till required. When the boil has reached the required degree pour the sugar on the slab, color it light green, and when partly cool, pull over the hook until it becomes a delicate satin tint; return it to the slab, press the boil out, lay the fondant paste in the centre and case it all around with the pulled sugar; now carefully work the one end of the boil down to a point as for [Pg 72] sticks and draw it out in lengths, required thickness: lay them on the machine and press gently until cut through; the buttercups are then ready for packing. It is advisable to work small boils of these goods, as the casing being boiled soon gets brittle; keep turning the bulk round on the plate so as to keep the fondant paste exactly in the centre.

RASPBERRY COCOANUT BUTTERCUPS.

7 lbs. Best White Sugar.
2 lbs. Fondant Paste.
1 lb Desiccated Cocoanut.
1 lb. Raspberry Jam, boiled Stiff.
1 teaspoonful cream of Tartar.
1 quart Water.
Carmine Color.
Borax.

Process. —Work the jam and cocoanut into the fondant paste; boil the sugar, water and cream tartar to crack; pour on oiled slab; color light rose tint: when partly cool, pull and work off as in the preceding recipe and cut with buttercup machine.

COCOANUT BUTTERCUPS.

7 lbs. Sugar.
2 lbs. Fondant Paste.
1 lb. Desiccated Cocoanut.
Yellow Color.
1 teaspoon Cream Tartar.
1 quart Water with Borax.
Lemon Flavor.

Process. —As usual, buttercups of any sort or flavor may be made by following the directions given, and substituting different essences, jams, chopped nuts or almonds, and color to fancy.

[Pg 73]

BLACK CURRANT BUTTERCUPS.

7 lbs. White Sugar.
2 lbs Fondant Paste.
1 lb. Black Currant Jam.
½ oz. Tartaric Acid.
1 teaspoonful Cream Tartar.
1 quart Water.
Borax.
Purple Color.

Process. —Work the jam, acid and color into the fondant paste, boil the sugar, water and cream tartar to crack, and work off as already described.

FONDANT CREAM WORK OR BUTTERCUP FILLING.

This branch of the business has developed wonderfully during the last few years. This cream is not only moulded and worked into every conceivable shape, size color and flavor by itself, but is used with chocolate, fruits, etc., to make an endless variety of pleasing and tasty confections. The smaller goods in this work form the body, and sometimes the whole, of many beautiful mixtures, and no window can now be considered orthodox unless they have a good display of these goods. For our purpose the variety is a matter of detail which we only mention to remind the reader that he must look for the greater part of it outside the covers of this guide. The process is practically the same all through; the mixing, flavors, colors and shapes make whatever distinction there is. It will only be necessary to give a fair selection of formulas to enable the reader to imitate anything he sees in this line, or invent something new.

[Pg 74]

Fig. 15. a
Asbestos Gas Batch Warmer or Spinnin 32 inches long, price $15.00. Can be use

RASPBERRY & VANILLA FONDANTS.

10 lbs. White Sugar.
2½ lbs. Glucose.
Raspberry and Vanilla Flavor.
3 pints water.
Carmine Color.

Process. —Boil the sugar, glucose and water in the usual way to the degree of soft ball; then remove the [Pg 75] pan from the fire; damp the pouring plate with cold water; pour the boil on it and let it remain till nearly cold. With a long pallette knife or wooden spatula, commence to work the syrup until it changes to a white glossy cream; then divide the batch into two; put one part in the pan and remelt it, just enough to make it a consistency to mould, add vanilla flavor and run it into rubber moulds; now put the other portion in the pan and remelt; color it a light pink; flavor with essence of raspberry and mould in the same shapes; when the goods are set and cold crystalize them with cold syrup.

N.B.—Have everything very clean when making fondants; every speck will show; a touch of blue will make the white a better color.

CHOCOLATE & VANILLA FONDANTS.

10 lbs White Sugar.
2½ lbs. Glucose.
Vanilla Flavoring.
3 pints Water.
½ lb. Pure Chocolate.

Process. —Prepare the fondant creams as in last recipe; when the boil has been creamed, divide into two, one part being twice the size of the other, put the small portion in the pan to remelt, adding the chocolate paste; stir until paste is dissolved and incorporated, but do not let the cream boil; remove the pan from the fire; run chocolate cream in rubber moulds filling the impressions only one-third part full; then melt the white cream, flavor with vanilla and fill up the moulds; when set crystalize in cold syrup; each fondant will be in two colors, white tipped with chocolate.

[Pg 76]
Fig. 15. Batch Warmer or Gas Candy H

COCOANUT FONDANTS.

9 lbs. White Sugar.
2½ lbs. Glucose.

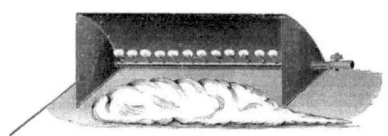

1½ lbs. Fine Desiccated Cocoanut, Unsweetened.
Carmine Color.
3 pints Water.
Lemon Flavoring.

Process.—Proceed to make the cream as before directed and divide the batch into two equal parts: remelt one part and stir in half the desiccated cocoanut with a few drops of lemon; half fill moulds; remelt the other portion of cream; stir in the remainder of the cocoanut; color pink, adding a few drops of essence lemon, and fill up the moulds; crystalize the usual way in cold syrup.

STRAWBERRY FONDANTS.

9 lbs. White Sugar.
2 lbs. Glucose.
Carmine Coloring.
2 lbs. Strawberry Jam.
3 pints Water.

Process.—Boil the sugar, glucose and water to a soft ball degree, pour the batch on pouring plate, which [Pg 77] has been previously damped with cold water, let the boil remain till nearly cold, then with a wooden spatula work the syrup about till it becomes cream, then mix in jam; return the whole to the pan and remelt, add sufficient color to make a bright pink, then run into moulds; when set, crystalize in cold syrup.

CHERRY FONDANTS.

10 lbs. Sugar.
2½ lbs. Glucose.
Cherry Flavor.
3 pints Water.
Carmine and Saffron Color.

Process.—Select some large, preserved cherries, cut them in half. Boil the sugar, glucose and water in the ordinary way to ball degree, pour the batch on a damp pouring plate; when nearly cold work up the whole with spatula till it becomes a white glossy cream, working the flavor in at the same time; then divide into three equal portions, color one portion a bright pink and another a yellow, leaving the third white; knead each portion into stiff paste, adding a little icing sugar to make it tough; pinch off small pieces and form them into balls about the size of the cherry, make them a little flat on one side; on this flat part stick a half cherry, squeezing them into shape; place them in canvas trays and put them in the drying room for a few hours to harden; afterwards crystalize with cold syrup. Other preserved fruits may be used in same way.

FONDANTS FOR MIXTURES.

10 lbs. White Sugar.
2½ lbs. Glucose.
Flavors Various.
3 pints Water.
Colors Various.
[Pg 78]

Process.—Boil the sugar, glucose and water as before directed to a stiff ball and pour the sugar on damp slab; let it stand till nearly cold, then work it up with spatula till glossy cream; divide the boil into as many portions as you want colors; then remelt this cream, color and flavor to fancy; run the batch into moulds of different shapes. When the fondants are set, crystalize in cold syrup. Fondants for mixture are made a trifle harder to prevent being crushed with other sweets with which they are mixed.

TO CRYSTALIZE FONDANTS

13 lbs. Best White Sugar.
4 pints Water.

Process.—Boil this quantity of sugar and water for a few minutes, about 220 degrees by the thermometer; stand it aside undisturbed till quite cold. Pack the fondants in crystalizing tins, putting wire trays between each layer of say two inches deep; let the wire trays take a bearing on the ends of the tin; when the tin is full, cover the goods with cold syrup, putting a damp cloth over the top; stand the tins in a cool place in the drying room about ten hours; then remove them to a cold place; about an hour afterwards take out the plugs and drain off the superfluous syrup; when the fondants are dry, turn the tins on end, giving them a slight knock and empty them on clean trays; they will be ready for packing in an hour or so.

N.B.—If a thin skin forms over the top of the syrup, skim it off before draining the goods; it may [Pg 79] tend to granulate them, but the damp cloth ought to prevent this skin forming.

CHRISTMAS FANCIES—CLEAR TOY MOULDS.

There are a great number of fancies made from grain sugars sold about Christmas time. Their beauty and attractiveness depends upon the moulds in which they are moulded, and the taste displayed in painting or decorating them. The goods themselves are quite a secondary consideration, being so simple to make.

Process.—Boil 7 lbs. sugar, 1 lb. glucose, 2 pints water in the usual way to the degree of ball 250, by thermometer; remove it from the fire and rub the sugar against the side of the pan until thick and white; stir it all together, then fill the moulds through the runner. Too much sugar must not be boiled at one time, or it will set before it can be all run into the moulds; two or three pounds will be enough for a beginner to practice with. They will be hard enough to be taken out of the moulds in fifteen to thirty minutes, according to size after being run, and they will be ready for decorating.

ARTIFICIAL FIGURES.

Fruit, eggs, and any object may be taken from nature by this process, to be transformed into sugar, afterwards glazed, colored to imitate nature so exactly as to deceive many persons. Boil the sugar in exactly the same way as directed in the previous recipe, grain [Pg 80] it and fill the moulds; in a few minutes run out as much sugar as will leave the mould; this will cause the casting to be hollow in the centre. Allow your articles to imitate the natural objects which they represent with liquid colors and camel's hair pencils; if gloss is required the colors should be mixed with a strong solution of gum arabic or isinglass to the desired tint.

COMPOSITION CLEAR TOY MOULDS.

Made from Finest Quality of Metal.

The Moulds marked thus X we have always in stock. Any others made to order.

	No.	Name.	No. in Mould.	No. to Lb.
x	1	Horse and Man large	3	16
x	2	Horse, small	3	48
x	3	General on Horse	3	27
x	4	Horse	4	45
	5	Horse, small	4	55
x	6	Cow	3	38
x	7	Sheep	4	30
x	8	Dog, large	3	43
x	9	Dog, medium	3	48
	10	Dog, small	3	55
x	11	Monkey on Horse	3	35
x	12	Cat, large	3	28
x	13	Cat, small	4	32
x	14	Rat	4	32
	15	Deer, small	3	32
	16	Camel	3	45
x	17	Rabbit, large	3	16
x	18	Rabbit, medium	4	24
x	19	Rabbit, small	4	38
x	20	Lady on Swan	3	30
	21	Chicken	3	38
x	22	Rooster	3	35
	23	Eagle	3	35
x	24	Crow	3	40
[Pg 81]	25	Bear	4	35
	26	Baby, large	3	32
	27	Baby, small	3	30
	28	Jim Crow	3	64
x	29	Man and Wheelbarrow	3	55
	30	Woman and Churn	4	48
	31	Hand	3	38
	32	Basket and Flowers	3	38
	33	Acorn	3	30
	34	Harp	3	31
x	35	Fireman	3	24
x	36	Tom Thumb	3	48
x	37	Soldier	4	48
	38	Steamboat	3	48
x	39	Locomotive	3	43
x	40	Sloop	3	43
	41	Flat Iron	4	48
	42	Key	3	35
	43	Skate	3	55
	44	Pistol	3	48
x	45	Shovel	3	27
	46	Scissors	3	43
	47	Fiddle	4	38
	48	Bugle	3	55
x	49	Watch	3	21
	50	Basket with handle	3	31
x	51	Flower Basket, handle	3	28
x	52	Pitcher, small	3	33
	53	Rocking Horse, small	3	35
x	54	Three Figures	3	48
x	55	Rabbit and Basket	4	16
x	56	Locomotive, large	3	14
x	57	Church on Hill	3	18
	58	Tea Pot	3	48
x	59	Lion	3	70
	60	Sword	3	27
	61	Boy and Goat	3	43
x	62	Watch, small	3	45
x	63	Donkey	3	55
	64	Elephant	3	43
	65	Caught in the Act	3	48
	66	Ladders	3	40
[Pg 82] x	67	Horse and Cart	3	28
x	68	Sparrow	3	19
	69	Small Boat	3	43
	70	Locomotive, small	3	28
	71	Pitchers	3	31
x	72	Sugar Bowl	3	21
	73	Tea Cup	3	40
x	74	Coffee Cup	3	21
	75	Saucers	3	35
x	76	Tea Pot	3	12
	77	Wine Glass	3	41
	78	Wash Tub	3	33
	79	Flower Vase	3	23
	80	Round Table	3	31
	81	Gun	4	48
	82	Pistol	4	32
	83	Pocket Knife	4	38
	84	Dirk	4	40
	85	Rooster, small	5	55
	86	Crucifix	5	32
	87	Axe	4	48
	88	Pipe	6	21
	89	Ass	5	48
x	90	Deer Lying Down	3	25
	91	Mule	3	21
x	92	Dog, large	3	12
x	93	Dog with Basket	3	12
x	94	Dog standing with Basket	3	15
x	95	Peacock	3	21
	96	Decanter	3	19
x	97	Boots	5	27
	98	Plain Basket with Handle	3	23
	99	Wine Glass, large	3	18
x	100	Fire Horn	3	21
	101	Squirrel and Box	5	33
	102	Broom	3	13
x	103	Bust of Napoleon	4	20
	104	Ladys	3	28
x	105	Cupid	3	21
	106	Rabbit	3	10
	107	Fish on Plate	3	19
x	108	Rooster	3	14

	No.	Item				No.	Item				No.	Item		
[Pg 83] x	109	Owl	3	16			Clothes			x	173	Railroad Car	3	18
						143	Pipe	6	33		174	Fancy Tea Kettle	3	11
x	110	Cupid and Basket	8	19	x	144	Sloop	3	12		175	Spread Eagle	2	7
					x	145	Rabbit and Wheelbarrow	3	6	x	176	Chinaman and Dog	3	13
x	111	Pony	3	18	x	146	Lamb, large	4	14		177	Rabbit Traveller	3	16
x	112	Dog	3	15	x	147	Monkey on Camel	3	8					
x	113	Cat and Dog Fighting	3	18	x	148	Boy and Large Lamb	3	11	x	178	Frog on Bicycle	3	15
	114	Grasshopper	3	13	x	149	Pig	3	18		179	Ostrich	3	12
x	115	Steamboat	3	19		150	Dog in Kennel	3	15		180	Tramp	3	12
x	116	Sea Lion	3	12	[Pg 84] x	151	Fancy Clock	3	18		181	Fox	2	12
x	117	Rhinoceros	3	15						x	182	Horse and Jockey	3	19
x	118	Tiger	3	15		152	Small Boy	3	30		183	Piggyback	3	16
x	119	Bear, small	3	20	x	153	Mazeppa	3	13		184	Fancy Pitcher, large	3	13
	120	Bear, Medium	3	16		154	Crane	3	15	x	185	Sail Boat	3	15
x	121	Bear, large	3	8		155	Squirrel	3	10	x	186	Irishman and Pig	3	15
x	122	Ape	3	14		156	Boy Riding Dog	3	18		187	Monkey and Piggyback	3	15
x	123	Large Hand	3	11		157	Goat Jumping	3	16					
x	124	Bear sitting up	3	16	x	158	Cow and Calf	3	23		188	Policeman and Boy	3	14
x	125	Camel	3	18		159	Organ Grinder with Monkey	3	24		189	Dog and Deer	3	12
x	126	Squirrel	3	13						x	190	Boy and Bicycle	3	18
	127	Horse Jumping	3	30		160	Chriskingle Deer and Sleigh	2	10		191	Owl on Tree	3	12
x	128	Lamb Lying Down	3	14	x	161	Basket	3	19		192	Puss in Boots	3	10
	129	Sugar Bowl	3	21	x	162	Baby in Cradle	3	16	[Pg 85] x	193	Kangaroo	3	11
	130	Double Pointed Iron	3	16	x	163	Horse	3	20	x	194	Giraffe	3	12
	131	Boy on Rocking Horse	3	19	x	164	Soldier Boy	3	13	x	195	Fancy Pipe	2	12
						165	French Lady	4	15	x	196	Rifle	4	38
	132	Elephant	6	21		166	Fancy Bottles	4	12		197	Irishman	3	23
	133	Captain Jack	3	18		167	Boy Stealing Apples	3	13	x	198	Chinaman	3	19
	134	Frog Smoking	3	16		168	Hussar	3	9	x	199	Israelite	2	10
	135	Swan	3	18		169	Scotchman	3	11		200	Uncle Sam	3	23
	136	Trumpet	3	16		170	Rabbit Soldier	3	9		201	Dutchman	3	16
	137	Boots	3	19		171	Rabbit Drummer	3	9	x	202	Dog Sitting Up	3	12
x	138	Elephant	3	14							203	Basket	3	14
x	139	Monkey on Camel	3	20	x	172	Rabbit Sportsman	3	16		204	Dog Running	3	21
x	140	Cupid on Lion	3	18							205	Shears	3	38
	141	Rabbit	4	25							206	Shovel	3	21
	142	Monkey Dressed in Soldier	3	24										

LARGE MOULDS FOR HOLLOW OR CLEAR TOYS.

No.	Name.	Size.	No. in Mould.	Pr
1	Deer	5 × 7	1	$4
2	Deer	3 × 7	1	2
3	Horse	5½ × 5½	1	6
*4	Horse	2½ × 2½	1	1
5	Horse	2½ × 2½	2	2
6	Horse	3 × 2½	1	1
*7	Horse	2 × 2½	3	2
*8	Camel	3 × 3	1	1
9	Camel	5½ × 5½	1	6
10	Elephant	3 × 5	1	2
11	Elephant and Boy	3 × 3	1	1
*12	Goat	3 × 2¾	2	2
*13	Cat	5 × 4½	1	2
14	Cat	3 × 4½	1	2
15	Dog	6 × 4	1	6
16	Dog Lying Down	3½ × 5½	1	2
17	Dog	3½ × 4½	2	3
18	Wm. Penn	5½ high	1	2
*19	Indian	5⅞ high	1	2
20	Rooster	5 × 3½	1	2
21	Rooster	3½ × 3	1	1
22	Locomotive	10 × 5½	1	1?
23 [Pg 86]	Locomotive, Rabbit Engineer	3½ × 3¾	1	2
24	Basket	2 × 6	1	9
25	Basket	4½ × 4	1	2
26	Priest Blessing Children	2 × 6	1	1
27	Washington	7 in. high	1	1
28	U. S. Grant	2¼ in. high	1	2
29	Gun	7 in. long	3	2
30	Gun	7 in. high	1	1
31	Ship Full Sail	7½ × 6	1	6
32	Steamboat	6½ × 4	1	6
33	Rowboat	9 in. long	1	4
34	Rowboat	6 in. long	1	1
*35	Rowboat	2½ in. long	2	2
36	Whistle		4	2
37	Whistle		3	1
38	Spread Eagle on Half Globe	4 × 6	1	6
39	Rabbit	5 × 5	1	2
40	Rabbit	3 × 3	2	2
*41	Lamb	4 × 6	1	2
42	Lamb	3¼ × 3½	2	2
43	Rowboat	4½ × 2½	1	2
44	Elephant, Jumbo	8½ × 6	1	6
45	Lion	8½ × 6	1	6
*46	Knight on Horseback	3 × 5½	1	1
47	Fire Engine	5 × 7	1	6
48	Buffalo	5½ × 8	1	6

VANILLA CREAM BARS.

7 lbs. White Sugar.
2 lbs. Glucose.
3 pints Water.
Vanilla Flavoring.

Process.—Dissolve the sugar with water in a clean pan; add the glucose and boil in the usual way to the degree of feather, 243; pour the contents on a damp slab; let it remain a few minutes to cool; then with a pallette knife work it up to white cream, adding a tint of blue to bleach it; when the whole has become a smooth cream, return it to the pan and melt it just sufficient that it may pour out smooth and level; stir in [Pg 87] the flavor and run on pouring plate ½ inch thick; when set cut into bars.

RASPBERRY OR ROSE CREAM BARS.

7 lbs. White Sugar.
2 lbs. Glucose.
3 pints Water.
Raspberry or Rose Flavor.

Process.—Melt the sugar in the water, add the glucose and boil to 243; pour contents on slab, and when cool divide the boil into three parts; color one part red, add some pure chocolate to another, and to a third add a pinch of blue, cream each part by rubbing on slab to a smooth paste; in rubbing in the pure chocolate, see that you have enough to make it a rich brown; for red portion use just sufficient to give a light rose pink. When all finished, melt each portion separately in the pan just sufficiently soft to run to a level surface; pour out first the red, then the chocolate on top of red sheet, then the white on top of chocolate; this will make a cream cake to cut up into bars. Some do not take the trouble to melt the cream, being satisfied to spread the paste out, smoothing it on top with a pallette knife; this answers the purpose but does not look so well.

COCOANUT CREAM.

7 lbs. White Sugar.
3 lbs. Cocoanut peeled and sliced.
2 lbs. Glucose.
Red Coloring.
3 pints Water.

Process. —Boil the sugar, glucose and water in the usual way to the degree 245; pour contents on slab; divide the boil into two lots; when cool, color one part [Pg 88] light pink and put a small touch of blue in the other; add the sliced cocoanut, half into each part, then commence to cream them by rubbing. When both parts have been mixed into a smooth paste, it is ready for sale, being usually sold by cutting from rough block.

N.B.—Cut almonds, ground walnuts, etc., are used in the same way as directed for cocoanuts. The boils may or may not be flavored, but a little improves it and makes it fragrant.

MAPLE CREAM.

8 lbs. Yellow Sugar.
1 quart Sweet Cream.
2 lbs. Glucose.

Process. —Boil the sugar, glucose and cream to 242 on thermometer, stirring all the time; when done lift off the fire and let stand till nearly cold (placing it where it will cool quickly), then stir until it sets; then melt over a slow fire (stirring constantly) until it becomes a nice creamy consistency, pour on a well greased tin, lay about one inch deep, let stand till cold, when by turning over the tin it will fall out. After the batch is set to cool in the tin, on no account disturb it as it will make the cream crack into pieces when turning out. If this is too expensive a recipe use milk instead of cream and add half a pound of butter.

CHRISTMAS PUDDING (IMITATION).

7 lbs. White Sugar.
1 lb. Raisins.
½ lb. Sweet Almonds blanched chopped.
1 lb. Currants.
1 lb. Sultanas.
½ lb. Mixed Peel.
1 oz. Mixed Spice.
2 pints Water.
 [Pg 89]

Process. —Prepare fruit by washing currants in cold water, afterwards drying them; stone raisins; blanch and chop almonds; cut the peel in stripes, then mix them together, adding the spice; boil the sugar and water to ball degree; remove the pan from the fire: grain the boil by rubbing the syrup against the side of the pan in the usual way; when it becomes creamy, add the mixed fruit, carefully stirring the whole until thoroughly incorporated; have some wet cloths ready, into which divide the boil; tie them very tight and hang them up until set hard. The blanched almonds are used to represent suet and should be chopped accordingly.

BROWN CREAM PUDDING.

7 lbs. Brown Sugar.
2 lbs. Glucose.
1 lb. Currants.
½ lb. Sultanas.
½ lb. Raisins.
½ lb. Mixed Peel.
½ oz. Mixed Spice.
2 pints Water.

Process. —Dissolve the sugar in the water and put the pan on the fire and add the glucose; let the whole boil to a stiff ball, then pour the contents on a damp pouring plate; when nearly cold commence to cream by rubbing and working it about the slab with pallette knife until it becomes opaque, stiff and creamy, have the fruit prepared and mix as in previous recipe, then work them into the boil with spatula; now divide the boil into small basins, holding about one pound each; press the cream well down and let them remain till set. Take them out, brush over them a thin solution of gum [Pg 90] and dust them with powdered sugar to represent frosting. Before putting the cream in the basins, shake a little icing sugar over the basins, it will keep them from sticking.

RASPBERRY NOYEAU.

5 lbs. White Sugar.
1 lb. Glucose.
2 lbs. Raspberry Jam.
1 lb. Almonds, blanched and Dried.
3 pints Water.
Liquid Brilliant Rose Color.

Process. —Boil the sugar, glucose and water to the ball degree, 250; ease the pan off the fire, add the jam and almonds, with sufficient color to make the whole a bright red; let the batch boil through, keeping it stirred gently until thoroughly mixed; now remove the pan from the fire and see if the batch has turned opaque; if not rub some of the syrup against the side of the pan and stir until whole boil shows a little creamy, then pour out on wafer paper, keeping the sheet about three-quarters of an inch thick; level the top down with pallette knife and cover with wafer paper; when set remove to a clean board and cut into bars with a sharp knife. In running sheets to thickness, arrange the loose bars on the pouring plate to form a square in proportion to the size of the boil. Almost any kind of jam can be substituted for flavoring Noyeau.

WHAT TO DO WITH SCRAPS AND SIFTINGS.

It is necessary to know how to use up the scraps, siftings, spoiled boil candies and otherwise unsaleable [Pg 91] goods. People who make jam or liquorice goods know of course what to do with them; but small makers often accumulate lots of waste which seems always in the way. This should be avoided as much as possible, not only on the ground of economy, but for the good order and general appearance of the workshop. Keep the acid scraps separate from the others; have two pans (earthenware will do) and make it a rule, when sweeping down the plates, to throw the acid scraps into one pan and the others into the second pan; keep them well covered with water, and, as the syrup then gets too thick, put in more water in order that the scraps may dissolve. When making dark goods such as cough candy, cough drops, cocoanut candy, stick jaw, etc., use a proportion of this syrup in each boil, dipping it out with a ladle. As a rule a careful workman would use up his scraps every day. Some use the machine scraps by putting them in the next boil when sugar is on the slab. The writer's experience is that that method is objectionable, as it not only causes the boil to be cloudy, but very often grains it. Melt the acid scraps in water enough to form a thin syrup; put in some whiting, powdered chalk or lime; put the pan on the fire and stir until whole boils; see that all the scraps are dissolved; remove the pan and let it stand for an hour, then strain through flannel. Use this syrup in the same way as the other for making common goods.

[Pg 92]

CREAM FOR CHOCOLATE CREAMS OR BARS.

10 lbs. White Sugar.
3 pints Water.
2½ lbs. Glucose.

Process. —Put the sugar, glucose and water in a clean pan and boil in the usual way until the batch reaches the degree of feather 245; (keep the sides of the pan free from sugar); pour out on damp pouring plate and let it remain till nearly cold; then with long pallette knife commence to rub the sugar against the plate and work it about until it changes from a clear syrup to snow white creamy substance; then knead it with the hand until of uniform softness and no lumps left in the mass; it is now ready for use and may be kept covered in stoneware jars until required for various purposes. In winter the sugar need not be boiled so high; in hot weather, a little higher. When packing the cream away in jars it is better to keep the top moist by laying on a damp cloth before putting in the cork. Seeing that cream keeps so well, of course it is saving to make much larger batches at a time. This can be easily arranged by multiplying the proportions according to size of pan and convenience. These proportions are a guide, but the writer knows of no absolute must be this or that, although he has made as many cream goods as most people and with as much success. He has seen as fine a sample made in the same workshop when the boil was made up a little different. However, in submitting his own formula, it may be taken for granted he is not a mile from the bull's eye.

[Pg 93]

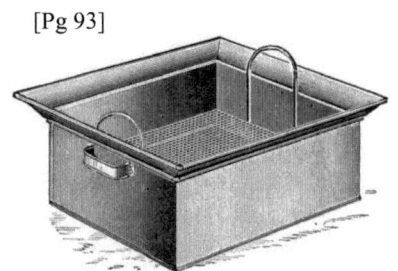

Fig. 17.
Chocolate Melter or Warmer.
No. 1 Size, 12½ × 14 × 6, price
No. 2 Size, 14¼ × 16½ × 6, "
Made from best quality of Tin Plate.

CHOCOLATE CREAM BUNS AND CAKES.

10 lbs. Sugar.
2½ lbs. Glucose.
3 pints Water.
½ oz. Vanilla Essence.

Process. —Boil the sugar, glucose and water in the ordinary way to the strong feather 245, then pour on damp slab, let it remain until nearly cold, add the flavor, and with pallette knife work up the boil till white and creamy; shape it with the hands or press into tin moulds; stand it in a warm place to harden a little on the outside. Melt some chocolate paste and cover the goods smoothly with it, using either knife or brush; when dry glaze them by brushing on a solution of shellac dissolved in alcohol.

[Pg 94]

N.B.—In this recipe the sugar is boiled higher than the "Cream for Chocolate Cream," because the goods are so large the soft cream would not keep in shape. In melting pure chocolate simply put it in a tin together with a piece of lard or cocoa butter, stand it near the fire, give it an occasional stir; it will soon dissolve; use no water or it will run to powder and be spoiled.

TAFFY PANS.
Per dozen, $1.25, $1.50, $1.75, $2.
SWINGING PANS.
We make any size to order.
CRYSTALIZING PANS AND WIRE TRAYS.
Extra Quality.

14 × 10 × 2½, complete $5.50.
COPPER CANDY LADLE.
No. 1, Fig. 7,

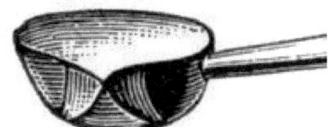

Fig. 7.

CHOCOLATE CREAM BARS No. 1.

10 lbs. White Sugar.
2½ lbs. Glucose.
Melted Chocolate.
3 pints Water.
Vanilla Flavor.

Process. —Prepare the cream as directed in Cream for Chocolate Cream, or use some of that cream. Have some tins with edges one and one-half inches deep; [Pg 95] grease some paper and fit it neatly round the sides and bottom. Melt some of the cream on a slow fire; flavor with Vanilla as soon as cream is sufficiently melted; remove the pan and pour contents into the tins to make a sheet about one inch thick or less. When set carefully empty, so as not to break the cake; have some melted chocolate and with a soft brush coat the cream on both sides; lay them on wires till cold and set; cut up into bars the required size. The knife for cutting bars of cream should be good, having a thin polished blade with a good edge. An old worn-out thing breaks the cream and makes it irregular.

COPPER CANDY DROP LADLE.
No. 2, Fig. 8, Price, $2.25.

CHOCOLATE CREAM BARS NO. 2.

10 lbs. White Sugar.
2½ lbs. Glucose.
Melted Chocolate.
3 pints Water.
½ oz. Essence Vanilla.

Process. —Prepare the tins by lining with greased paper, fitting them smoothly; melt some sweet chocolate paste and pour it about a quarter of an inch thick on the bottom of the tins; when set prepare some cream as directed for "Cream for Chocolate Cream," or use [Pg 96] some of that cream, melting it over a slow fire (do not allow it to boil); stir in the extract of vanilla and pour the batch in tins about one inch deep: when set, coat on top with melted sweet chocolate; when this lot is cold and quite set, cut up into bars with a sharp knife.

CHOCOLATE DROPS, PLAIN.

Warm some sweet chocolate; when it is just sufficiently heated to be pliable, pinch off little pieces, roll them in the hands to size of a small marble; place them in rows on sheets of white paper, each row about an inch apart; when the sheet is covered, take it by the corners and lift it up and down, letting it touch the slab each time; this will flatten the balls into drop shapes; they should be about the size of a ten cent piece on the bottom; when cold they will slip off the paper without any trouble.

[Pg 97]

CHOCOLATE DROPS (NONPAREIL.)

Process exactly as for plain drops. When the drops have been flattened, cover the sheets of paper entirely over with white nonpareil (hundreds and thousands); when the drops are dry shake off the surplus ones.

CHOCOLATE CREAMS.

Melt some cream (see "Cream for Chocolate Cream") use the runner and fill the moulds; in an hour the cream will be set hard enough to be taken out of the moulds; they are then ready for coating. Warm some sweet chocolate paste until melted, then drop the creams into the melted chocolate, two or three at a time; lift them out with a long fork and place them on glazed paper or sheets of tin to dry; put them in a cool place to harden; pack carefully in paper lined boxes in such a manner that they hardly touch each other; if packed roughly like most other candies, they become spotted and rough, spoiling the appearance altogether.

Rubber moulds are now largely used for making these goods; being much cleaner and very much easier used than starch moulds, and for new beginners are very much better than starch. These moulds are now to be bought much cheaper than they were a few years ago, the price now being about $1.40 per lb. These moulds weigh about two pounds each and hold ninety chocolate drops and can be refilled every half hour. We would strongly advise the purchase of rubber [Pg 98] moulds, as besides the saving of time, neither starch boards, starch, plaster moulds or bellows are required. Fletcher Manfg Co., carry a full line of moulds for chocolates and creams.

CHOCOLATE FOR DIPPING.

This mixing is so often required by confectioners for so many purposes that a good general recipe will not be out of place. If the instructions are followed and a little discretion used with the colors, a light glossy chocolate coating will be the result.

1 lb. Pure Chocolate.
3 oz. White Wax.
Chocolate Brown Color.
Cochineal.

Process. —Put the chocolate in a saucepan; stand on the furnace plate or near a fire; break up the wax into little pieces and stir it in until all is melted; then add the brown color, with a little liquid cochineal, stirring the whole until thoroughly mixed; it is then ready for use. For cheap common goods, more wax may be used. When mixing in the color try a little on a piece of white paper until satisfied with the blend.

GELATINE COCOANUT BARS (YELLOW).

8 lbs. White Sugar.
6 lbs. Glucose.
2½ lbs. Gelatine.
3 lbs. Cocoanut sliced.
1 oz. Acid Tartaric.
3 pints Water.
Saffron Color.
Lemon Flavor.

Process.—Soak the gelatine in cold water for twelve hours, boil the sugar, glucose and water to a [Pg 99] stiff ball, 255; remove the pan from the fire; stir in the gelatine till dissolved; let it stand for a few minutes and remove the scum from the top, then add the acid, flavor and cocoanut; gently stir the whole until well mixed; tinge a bright yellow with saffron; pour into oiled tins, making the sheet ½ inch thick; when set, cut up in sticks to sell two or four for a cent.

N.B.—This boil may be divided into two lots, one half colored red and flavored, raspberry, or a second boil may be made precisely as this one altering the color and flavor only.

PATENT RUBBER CANDY MOULDS

New Patterns.

The best process in the world for making moulded Bon-bons or French Creams and grained work, is by using Patent Rubber Candy Moulds. They will entirely supplant the use of starch as a mould for manufacturing such candies for the following reasons.

I.—Not alone can all the patterns at present made in starch be reproduced in these moulds but also a large variety of others with a perfection not before known, and which it would be impossible to use in starch.

II.—A much superior quality of goods is produced, in as much as the candies show as perfect a pattern as the moulds themselves.

III.—A saving at least 33 per cent is accomplished in labor.

IV.—No starch boards or starch is required, consequently the filling, printing, sifting and blowing off are dispensed with—six items of expense.

V.—The moulds specially facilitate the making of cream walnuts, cream almonds and cream jellies and other combinations, because the nuts, etc., can be pressed on the candy as soon as it has been poured into the moulds. This cannot be done with starch moulds, as any pressure on those will destroy the pattern.

[Pg 100]

VI.—Casting into starch moulds requires considerable experience and skill in order to do work well, while any workman can turn out the most perfect work with the rubber moulds, without any previous experience in such work.

VII.—A saving of room is effected, as a starch room is not required and the capacity of the rubber moulds is so much greater than starch boards of equal size that a comparatively less number of moulds are required to produce an equal quantity of goods.

VIII.—No starch being used, the shop will remain much cleaner.

These moulds are made of Pure Para Rubber and will, with proper usage last from twelve to fifteen years, judging from those which have been in use for the past four years.

An objection which naturally suggests itself to a person who has never tried these moulds, is that the candies might possibly have some taste of the rubber. This is not the case, however.

NOT THE SLIGHTEST TASTE OF RUBBER

is discernable. Not one of our many customers, either in this city or throughout the country, has made a single complaint. This proves that there is absolutely no difference between candies made in rubber moulds and candies made in starch moulds.

The demand for these moulds increases every year.

WRITE FOR PRICES AND PARTICULARS.

Cream to be run in these moulds should be cooked one degree lower than usual for starch.

Crystal ½ degree lower than usual for starch.

Before using New Moulds for first time, soak for half an hour in strong common washing soda and water.

CHEAP JELLY GOODS.

14 lbs. White Sugar.
12 lbs. Glucose.
3 lbs. Gelatine.
Flavor.
2 oz. Tartaric Acid.
2 pints water.
Color.

Process.—Soak the gelatine in cold water for twelve hours; bring the sugar, and water to a boil, [Pg 101] then add the glucose and continue boiling till it reaches the degree of stiff ball; remove the pan from the fire and stir in the gelatine and acid till dissolved; color and flavor to fancy; remove the scum and run the batch into tins. Set the goods aside for twelve hours, then cut up into jubes and crystalize with fine powdered sugar. This is a cheap line; there is not much body in them, but they sell at a price and give satisfaction.

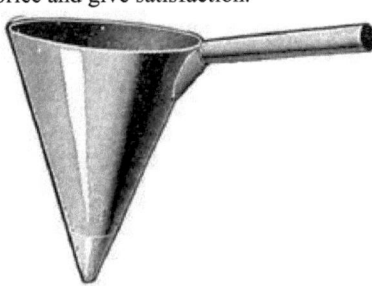

Funnel Droppers.

		Tin.	Copper.
No.	0	40	75
"	1	60	1.25
"	2	90	1.50

JELLY FANCIES.

12 lbs. Sugar.
7 lbs. Glucose.
3 pints Water.
3 lbs. Gelatine.
2 oz. Tartaric Acid.

Process.—Soak gelatine in cold water for twelve hours. Boil the sugar, glucose and water in the usual way to the degree of ball; remove the pan from the [Pg 102] fire and stir in the gelatine gradually until dissolved; let it stand for a few minutes; take off the scum as it rises, then divide the boil, if required in more than one, color and flavor each portion to fancy, then run the boil in the moulds; when set put them on clean slab, sprinkle some cold water over them and roll them about until all are damped, then cover them with fine crystal sugar and mix them up till crystalized all over, and spread them out on trays to dry.

The different recipes already given will give the reader a general idea how gelatine goods are made. By using different colors, flavors and shapes an infinite variety can be produced. It would serve no good purpose to further multiply these formulas for small goods.

JAM ROLEY POLEY.

10 lbs. White Sugar.
5 lbs. Glucose.
2 lbs Gelatine.
Carmine Color.
1 lb. Raspberry Jam.
1 lb. Desiccated Cocoanut.
3 pints Water.

Process. —Soak the gelatine in cold water for twelve hours; boil the sugar, glucose and water sharply to stiff ball; remove the pan from the fire, stir in the gelatine, stand aside till scum rises and skim it off; divide the boil into two portions, (mix together 1 oz. tartaric acid, 1 oz. carbonate of soda, 2 oz. icing sugar); drop this powder and the desiccated cocoanut into one half of the boil and stir briskly until the whole rises in a white foam, then run out into tins, on sheet about ¼ [Pg 103] inch thick; now take the other half, color bright red, adding the raspberry jam; stir till thoroughly mixed and run this on top of the white sheet about the same thickness; when cold and hard, take out the sheets and make a roll of each.

N.B.—Let the red portion be cool when run over the white, as the white being lighter will come to the top if disturbed by the mixture being too hot.

RASPBERRY JELLIES.

9 lbs. White Sugar.
6 lbs. Glucose.
2 lbs. Apple Jelly.
2¼ lbs. Gelatine.
3 pints Water.
2 oz. Tartaric Acid.
½ oz. Essence Raspberry.
Carmine Color.

Process. —Soak the gelatine as usual; boil the sugar, glucose and water to a stiff ball; remove the pan from the fire; stir in the gelatine and let it remain till scum rises; skim it off, then add jelly, acid and flavor and sufficient color to make a bright red: now mould the batch into Raspberry shapes and put them in a cold place. When set stiff, put the goods in thin layers in a crystalizing tin and cover them with cold syrup. Let them remain undisturbed for twelve hours, then drain off all the surplus syrup and turn the raspberries on clean trays; when dry, pack.

N.B.—When putting jelly goods in tins, be careful that the layers are not thick, as they lay so close that the syrup cannot get in between them. A good plan is to have wire trays and fix three or four loosely in each [Pg 104] tin, taking their bearings on the ends of the crystalizing tin. By this means you will get more in a tin with better result. Boil the syrup in the proportion of six pounds best white sugar to each quart water, to the degree of smooth 215. It must be quite cold when used for gelatine work or the goods will come out of the tins in a solid block.

BLACK CURRANT JELLIES.

9 lbs. White Sugar.
6 lbs. Glucose.
2¼ lbs. Gelatine.
Purple Coloring.
3 pints Water.
2 oz. Tartaric Acid.
2 lbs. Black Currant Jelly.

Process. —Soak gelatine as usual, smooth off and mould fondant shapes. Boil the sugar, glucose and water, as already directed, to a stiff ball; remove the pan from the fire, drop in the gelatine, a few pieces at a time, stir till dissolved. Let it remain a short time till the scum rises; skim it off, then stir in the tartaric acid, jelly and sufficient color to make the mixture a bright color, then mould the batch. When the goods are firmly set, place them in layers on wire frames fitted for crystalizing pan; arrange the frames in the tins and cover with cold syrup; let them stand for twelve or fourteen hours undisturbed, then drain off the surplus syrup; take them carefully out of the tins, pack them on clean trays; when dry they are ready for boxing. These goods require handling gently; they are very delicate and easily crushed.
[Pg 105]

PINEAPPLE JELLIES.

8 lbs. White Sugar.
8 lbs. Glucose.

2¼ lbs. Gelatine.
Pineapple Flavor.
3 oz. Tartaric Acid.
3 pints Water.
Saffron Color.

Process. —Soak the gelatine in sufficient cold water to cover it. Boil the sugar, glucose and water as usual to stiff ball and remove the pan from the fire; stir in the gelatine, wait till scum rises and remove it; then add the acid, flavor and sufficient color to make bright yellow; pour the mixing into pineapple moulds; [Pg 106] keep them in a cold place till set; pack them in layers in wire frames; put them in the crystalizing tins and cover with cold syrup; stand aside where they will not be shaken or disturbed for twelve or fourteen hours; then draw off the surplus syrup and put them in clean trays to dry. In flavoring these goods, use the pineapple gently, only a few drops, too much spoils them.

[Pg 107]
Kingery's Perfection Steam Power Coffee and Peanut Roaster and Warmer.

Size and Style of Machine we carry in stock marked thus*

			With Steam Whistle.
1	Peck Size, Tin Warmer	$100 00	$104 00
*1	Peck Size, Copper Warmer	108 00	112 00
2	Peck Size, Tin Warmer	115 00	119 00
2	Peck Size, Copper Warmer	124 00	128 00
1	Bushel Size, Tin Warmer	135 00	139 00
1	Bushel Size, Copper Warmer	148 00	152 00

Fletcher's "UNCLE SAM" Dry Air Peanut Warmer.
Japanned and Ornamented Glass Front.
Size—1 foot 7 in. × 1 foot 5 in., 1 foot 10 in. high.
Price complete $6 50

BEST WAY TO CRYSTALIZE GUM GOODS.
13 lbs. Best White Sugar.
2 quarts Water.

Process. —Have the goods cleaned and put in crystalizing tins; bring the above quantity of sugar and water just to the boil and stand aside until only milk warm; then pour it gently over the goods until covered; then slip the hands into the middle of the goods, and with the fingers just ease this bulk so that the syrup will flow freely between them; withdraw the hands [Pg 108] carefully and cover the tin; do not again disturb it for the next twelve hours, when the goods will be ready to drain and dry. To an experienced man, this method may seem a little dangerous and likely to spoil the crystal; but it will not do so if done carefully. Of course, it is understood the goods are not to be roughly stirred up, but simply loosened.

Concentrated Flower and Essence Flavors for Confectioners.

ESPECIALLY ADAPTED FOR FINEST WORK.

Essence	Maraschino.
"	Pistachio.
"	Ratafia.
"	Lilly of the Valley.
"	Dainty.
"	French Rose.
"	Ylang Ylang.
"	Patchouli.
"	Tuberose.
"	Carnation.
"	Heliotrope.
"	Crabapple.
"	Jasmine.
"	Millifleurs.
"	Hyacinth.
"	Cachou.
"	Bon-Tons.
"	Mirabells.
"	Sweet Briar.
"	Locust Flower.
"	Lilac Blossoms.
"	Fleur de Raisin.

"   Apple Blossom.
"   Violet (True).
"   Wood Violet.
"   Orange Blossom.
"   Hawthorne.
"   Wild Olive.
"   Musk.

Flavoring Extracts.

Extract   Currant.
"   Jamaica Ginger.
"   Gooseberry.
"   Grape.
"   Lemon.
"   Mead.
"   Nectar.
"   Orris.
"   Cinnamon.
"   Quince.
"   Rose.
"   Strawberry.
"   Anisette.
"   Apple.
"   Apricot.
"   Banana.
"   Bitter Almonds.
"   Blackberry.
"   Catawba.
"   Cherry.
"   Plum.
"   Raspberry.
"   Sarsaparilla.
"   Wintergreen.

Essential Oils.
Best Qualities.

Our Essential Oils will be found equal to anything obtainable. Write us for prices on anything you require. We cater especially to the candy makers and confectioners.

FLETCHER MNF'G. CO.
    440 & 442 Yonge Street,
        Toronto, Ont.
[Pg 109]

FLETCHER MNF'G. CO.

Importers and Dealers in

Confectioners Colors, Flavoring Extracts, Concentrated Fruit Oils, Flower Essences, Fine Essential Oils, Soluble Extracts, etc., for Bakers and Confectioners.

PURE FRUIT JUICES

prepared by newly discovered process, keep any length of time corked or uncorked in any temperature.
FLETCHER Mnf'g Co.
    440 & 442 Yonge St,
        Toronto.
[Pg 110]

PURE MALT EXTRACT.

Largely used by Bakers to prevent Bread from becoming dry, and to give it a sweet and nutty Flavor. It ensures shorter and sounder Fermentation.

BREAD made with it is easily digested, makes larger loaves, golden tinged crust, general satisfaction to the Consumer and profit to the Baker.
        AGENTS,
FLETCHER Mnf'g. Co.
    440 & 442 Yonge St,
        Toronto.
[Pg 111]

FLETCHER MNF'G. CO.
TORONTO

CANADIAN AGENTS FOR

THE CELEBRATED XXXX BRAND OF GLUCOSE

Guaranteed Equal, if not Superior, to any on the Market.

Its uniform high quality, good color and great specific gravity, has created for it such a reputation that orders could not be filled, this season, as fast as required; is now largely used by the best wholesale and retail confectioners of Canada. With our repeat orders we have some very flattering testimonials as to its high quality. Our Prices are Right. The goods when once tried need no other recommendation.

Sold in barrels, half, quarters and pails.

Samples and prices on application.
FLETCHER MNF'G. CO.
    Toronto.

[Pg 112]

Our LEADING SPECIA
fountains.

We make liberal allowances for old a EASY TERMS OF PAYMENT.

Transcriber's Note

Misspelled words have been corrected. Punctuation in this book is somewhat erratic; in general, this has not been altered from the original. However, when punctuation clearly follows a specific pattern, punctuation has been standardized.

In the recipe for ACID DROPS AND TABLETS, the original wording says to "add the acid which has been finally powdered." Since this seems like a typo, it has been changed to "finely powdered."

In the table of COMPOSITION CLEAR TOY MOULDS, the ones digit of the "No. per lb." is unreadable for items 34 (Harp), 35 (Fireman), and 46 (Scissors). The numbers listed in that column for those items are guesses.

In the recipe for TAR COUGH DROPS, the tar referred to is probably pine tar.